A is for Armageddon

aye ·· iz ·· fore ·· arrgh · ma · ged · don — A catalogue of disasters that may culminate in the end of the world as we know it. Have a nice day.

A
Armageddon
(666)

Richard Horne

HARPER

NEW YORK · LONDON · TORONTO · SYDNEY

In loving Memory
— of —

THE HUMAN RACE

HARPER

A IS FOR ARMAGEDDON. Copyright © 2009 by Richard Horne. All rights reserved. Printed in the United States of America. No part of this book may be used or reproduced in any manner whatsoever without written permission except in the case of brief quotations embodied in critical articles and reviews. For information address HarperCollins Publishers, 10 East 53rd Street, New York, NY 10022.

HarperCollins books may be purchased for educational, business, or sales promotional use. For information please write: Special Markets Department, HarperCollins Publishers, 10 East 53rd Street, New York, NY, 100222.

FIRST U.S. EDITION

Library of Congress Cataloging-in-Publication data is available upon request.

ISBN 978-0-06-200593-9

11 12 13 14 15 QGT 10 9 8 7 6 5 4 3 2 1

This book belongs to

....

☐ a fantasist   ☐ an optimist   ☐ a realist
☐ a pessimist   ☐ a doommonger

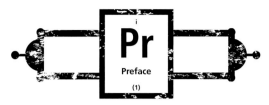

Preface. *preface* – the beginning of the end.

A is for Armageddon is a catalogue of a catalogue of disasters that are ready to befall the Earth and ultimately the human race. It has been designed, illustrated and written to give a concise guide of what to expect in the coming days, months, years and centuries. The book covers subjects that are way beyond our control,[1] issues that have been caused or accelerated, directly or indirectly, by humankind's many busy hands[2] and other situations that are just plain ridiculous.[3] Written, illustrated and designed with an optimistically pessimistic twang, *A is for Armageddon* highlights what you should be looking out for, when you should be panicking, and just how long you've got before we're all due to visit the big dead dodo sanctuary in the sky.

The world is a very complicated place and what follows is a snapshot of some of the many pitfalls that may befall Earth and the human race. In one case, a single scenario may be enough to finish us off, whereas it may take a combination of little disasters to create a truly huge one.

The idea for *A is for Armageddon* came after I'd completed my first, and very optimistic book, *101 Things To Do Before You Die* in late 2004. What followed was the design and concept of the 'Periodic Catastrophic',[4] a periodic table based in disaster, and a truly disastrous project was born.

Since I began work on the project, biblical-style natural disasters have occurred, tensions between nuclear countries have resurfaced, satellites have begun colliding and falling from space, economies have crunched, crumbled and collapsed, species have disappeared, a potential pig pandemic caused pandemonium, the terrifying climate of fear through terrorism has hotted up while our actual climate has heated up further towards an irreparable tipping point.

So whatever you believe in, whether you put your faith in an unseen omnipresent god or faith in science that states the Universe became something from nothing, we can all believe that it may be the beginning of the end of the world as we know it.

The armchair science of *A is for Armageddon* has never been more important to you than it is now, as things could start to get a little messy.

---

1. *See* Asteroid collision (224), Black holes (222) and Acts of God (48) • 2. *See* Melting glaciers (70), Deforestation (120) and Temperature rise (104) • 3. *See* Planet X (250), Mayan calendar: 2012 (146) and Grey goo (158) • 4. *See* Over

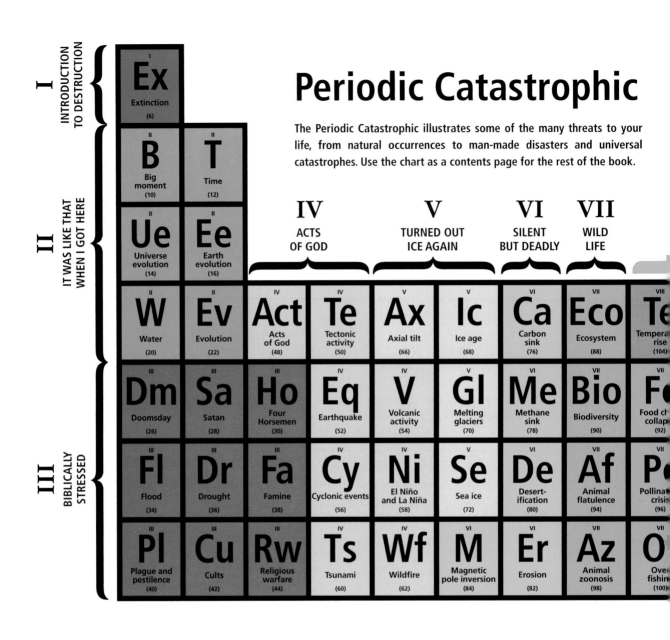

Periodic Catastrophic

The Periodic Catastrophic illustrates some of the many threats to your life, from natural occurrences to man-made disasters and universal catastrophes. Use the chart as a contents page for the rest of the book.

I — INTRODUCTION TO DESTRUCTION

Ex Extinction (6)	

II — IT WAS LIKE THAT WHEN I GOT HERE

III — BIBLICALLY STRESSED

IV — ACTS OF GOD

V — TURNED OUT ICE AGAIN

VI — SILENT BUT DEADLY

VII — WILD LIFE

B Big moment (10)

T Time (12)

Ue Universe evolution (14)

Ee Earth evolution (16)

W Water (20)

Ev Evolution (22)

Act Acts of God (48)

Te Tectonic activity (50)

Ax Axial tilt (66)

Ic Ice age (68)

Ca Carbon sink (76)

Eco Ecosystem (88)

Te Tempera... rise (104)

Dm Doomsday (26)

Sa Satan (28)

Ho Four Horsemen (30)

Eq Earthquake (52)

V Volcanic activity (54)

Gl Melting glaciers (70)

Me Methane sink (78)

Bio Biodiversity (90)

Fo Food ch... collap... (92)

Fl Flood (34)

Dr Drought (36)

Fa Famine (38)

Cy Cyclonic events (56)

Ni El Niño and La Niña (58)

Se Sea ice (72)

De Desert- ification (80)

Af Animal flatulence (94)

P... Pollinat... crisis (96)

Pl Plague and pestilence (40)

Cu Cults (42)

Rw Religious warfare (44)

Ts Tsunami (60)

Wf Wildfire (62)

M Magnetic pole inversion (84)

Er Erosion (82)

Az Animal zoonosis (98)

O... Over fishin... (100)

XV — UNIVERSALLY DOOMED

Uni Death of the Universe (218)

G Gravity (220)

Blk Black hole (222)

As Asteroid collision (224)

Mn Moon (228)

S... Sun (230)...

Mu Multiverse (236)

Pa Paradox (238)

Cc Collapse of causality (240)

Vc Vacuum metastability (242)

Sd Space dust (244)

A... Alien (246)

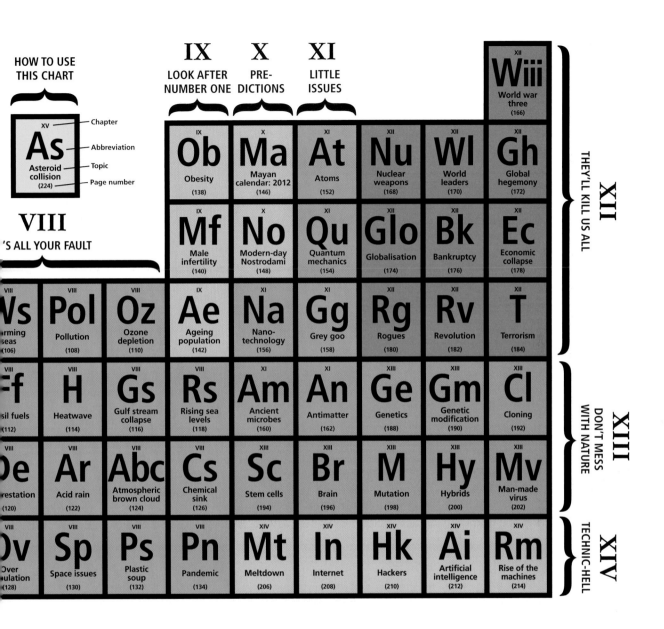
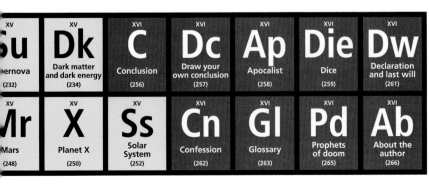

I

Introduction
to destruction

Introduction to destruction. *in·trow·duck·shon··to··dis·truck·shon* – the beginning of the end.

For billions of years, our Earth has been subjected to various forms of abuse. It has been beaten and bruised, stoned and scorched, disembowelled and dismembered. But Earth has lived to tell the tale, unlike many of the species that have inhabited it.

And while Earth may continue to survive multiple assassination attempts, the human race will not. No one knows exactly when or how our lineage is due to end[1] but our end is definitely nigh, and once we've gone, the Earth will still be here waiting for the next infestation to take control of its surface. So as we are all destined to die anyway, let's laugh in the face of extinction and hope that Death has forgotten to pencil in Judgment Day on his To Do list.

---

1. If we did, then we'd have bankrupted all the bookies of the world by now

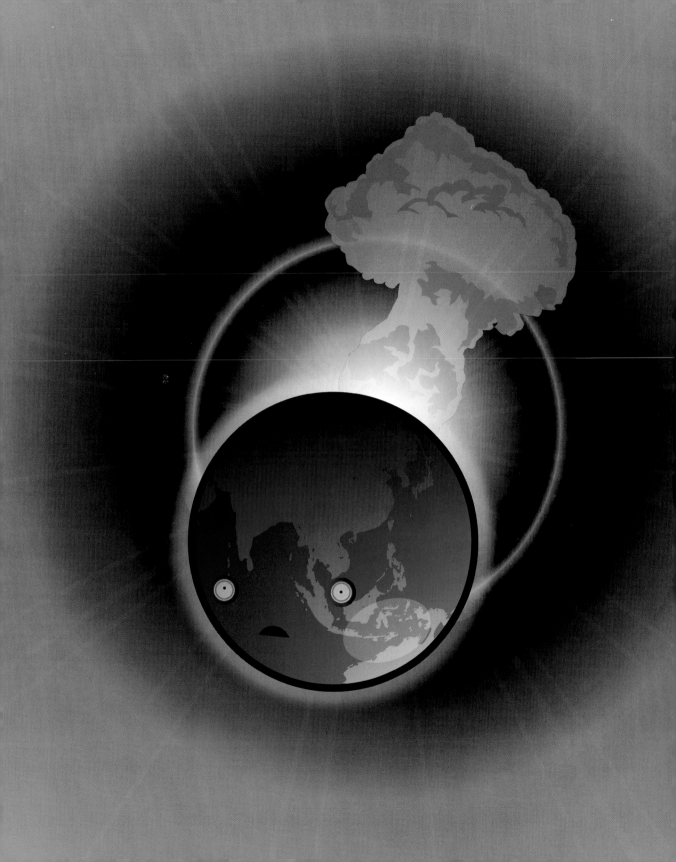

Ex

Extinction

(6)

Extinction. *x·ting·shon* – when you and the six billion people that are a similar size and shape to you no longer exist.

Humankind has been walking the tightrope of extinction ever since its conception, when that first single-celled organism got bored of being on its own and created an identical friend from itself. The long journey to reach the current stage of evolution has been a minefield of chance, circumstance and various catastrophic events that have tried to wipe our race off the face of the planet. Our ancestors managed to ramble their way successfully through the minefield, while other unlucky species, like our Neanderthal cousins, marched confidently into countless booby traps and were dispatched to the great retirement zoo in the sky. As for the human race, extinction is not an option. With the help of our scientific minesweepers,[1] we're attempting to survive Earth's evolutionary war zone for as long as possible without our entire unit being completely annihilated.

WHEN WILL IT HAPPEN?

Maybe not today, maybe not tomorrow, but soon. As everything is out to get us,[2] it's just a question of what will finish us off first.

WHAT'S LEFT?

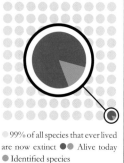

Source: Figures based on WWF estimates

99% of all species that ever lived are now extinct ●● Alive today ● Identified species

WHEN SHOULD I START TO PANIC?

WHAT SHOULD I LOOK FOR?

Keep a look-out for killer asteroids, violent storms, rising sea levels, sun expansion, disease, famine, fire, drought, war, a choking atmosphere ... the list is pretty long. Be afraid, be very afraid ...

POSSIBILITY IT WILL HAPPEN?

100% – change is inevitable. Roll with the punches and remember that there's always safety in numbers.

WHAT SHOULD I DO NEXT?

Space arks should be built to preserve what's left of the Earth's bio-diversity.[3] They must remain in orbit until the Earth is refurbished for their eventual re-introduction. In man's absence, monkeys are to be placed in charge of the arks.

---

1. Asteroid detectors, disease screenings, vaccinations, defence against alien invasion, etc • 2. Including fellow humans (trust no one) • 3. The animals went into space two by two ...

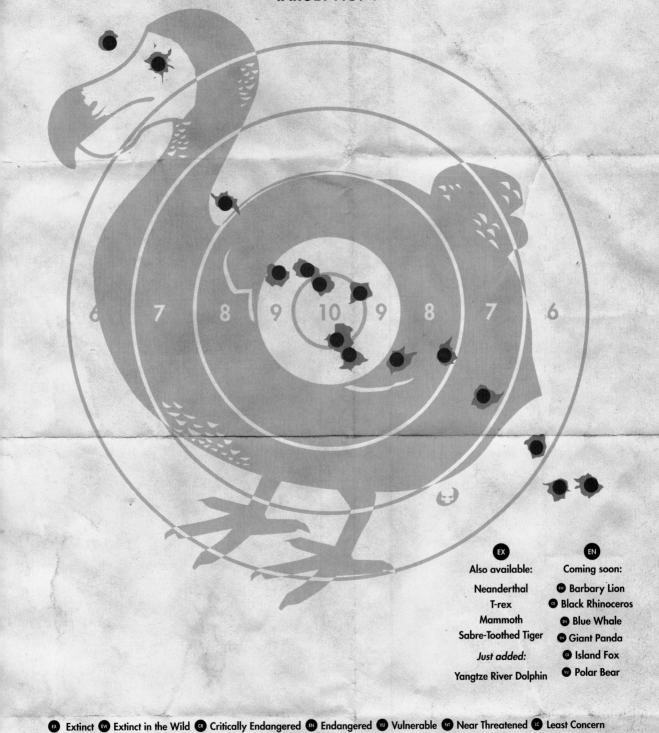

DODO
EXTINCTION SERIES

TARGET NO. 4

6 7 8 9 10 9 8 7 6

Also available:

Neanderthal

T-rex

Mammoth

Sabre-Toothed Tiger

Just added:

Yangtze River Dolphin

Coming soon:

Barbary Lion

Black Rhinoceros

Blue Whale

Giant Panda

Island Fox

Polar Bear

EX Extinct EW Extinct in the Wild CR Critically Endangered EN Endangered VU Vulnerable NT Near Threatened LC Least Concern

II

It was like that when I got here

It was like that when I got here. *it··woz··lyke··that··wen··eye ··got··hear* – don't blame me, I didn't do it. It's not my fault.

Over the last 13.7 billion years, since the very beginning of the known Universe, a complex series of events has occurred which has ultimately led to you, a unique human being. But for all this effort the Universe doesn't care for you: you're just a part of a bigger machine, another cog in the Universe's complicated mechanism. And while humankind is responsible for many of the world's current troubles and possibly its own ultimate destruction, the Universe was functioning perfectly well before we got here and it'll carry on with or without us perfectly well until its number comes up.[1]

But to understand why humankind is going to come to an end, we need to go back to the very beginning ... a very good place to start.

---

1. *See* Death of the Universe (218)

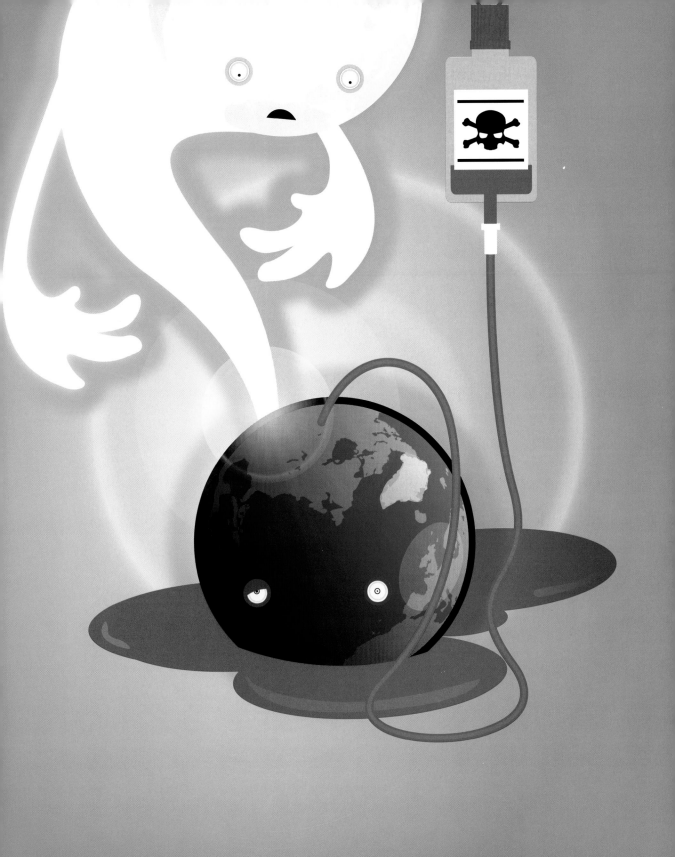

B
Big moment
(10)

Big moment. *big··mo·ment* – when nothing became everything.

Before everything, there was nothing – then nothing became something and when this something arrived, it announced itself with a very BIG bang. This 'something' turned out to be the single most explosive episode in the history of the Universe. Every single thing that has happened in the big void that we live in pales into insignificance in comparison to this one very BIG moment. This massive explosion set the events in motion that eventually created the Heavens and the Earth and we're very grateful for that, as it isn't easy to create life from a pile of junk left over from a massive nuclear explosion. Take a trip to Chernobyl, rummage through the radioactive debris and try for yourself.[1]

The Universe is a big and mysterious place which won't give up its secrets easily. The big bang is the best theory about how the Universe came into being[2] but questions still remain: What triggered it? What happened before it went boom? If a massive explosion created the Universe, is it possible that a similar explosion will destroy it? And since we came from nothing will we go back to nothing?[3] While we wait for our questions to be processed and our ultimate fate to be worked out, we're thankful that our little corner of the cosmos seems currently to be behaving itself, even though we know it's only a matter of time before the Universe sends us a reminder that we're small and insignificant in the form of a relatively tiny pebble[4] or maybe in the form of a catastrophically large rip.[5] Our time is running out on this rock and this rock is probably going to run out of Universe.

WHAT SHOULD I LOOK FOR?	WHEN SHOULD I START TO PANIC?	OPTIMISTIC VIEW OF EXISTENCE
A rapidly shrinking solar system displaying unusual activity in the night sky, consisting of the following: fire, blinding bright lights, fierce rushing winds, deafening noise and a feeling of falling.		I am made of star dust, as is everything else in the Universe. **PESSIMISTIC VIEW OF EXISTENCE** I am made of space trash from the detritus of the big bang.

1. *Do not* try this for yourself • 2. Some may disagree, *see* Acts of God (48) • 3. *See* Death of the Universe (318) • 4. *See* Asteroid collision (224) • 5. *See* Vacuum metastability (242)

BaNG

Do not try this
for yourself

Time (12)

Time. *tyme* – the measurements of one seco

Time has been a constant pain in humankind's coll
t was first perceived to exist. The fact that it is a
doesn't really exist hasn't stopped people from r
to kill Time. After years of experimenting, it was
successful way to dispose of it is to have plenty of
you let Time fly, you'll have less of a shot at it. Stra
how many times you kill it, Time will never die. A
leave a stitch, or nine, in Time but this won't ha
stop it from ebbing away. Not only can it not be k
or save time are also futile. Time, it seems, is a pa
and running out, even though tick will always
uncertain future for humankind's evolutionary lin
Only Time will tell.

WHEN WILL IT HAPPEN?

Time is constantly marching, but don't lag behind as time (and tide) waits for no one. Every tick and tock of the clock takes its toll on your own internal ticker. This next second could be your last so seize the moment and hold it to ransom without delay.

WHAT SHOULD I LOOK FOR?

Two-timers, signs of ageing, Time bombs, the sands of Time slipping through your fingers.

WHEN SHOULD I START TO PANIC?

LATER | TOO LATE | SOON | NOW

You've been living on borrowed Time from the very moment you were born, so there's no point panicking. Once you realise that Death has you in his sights, think about ways you can cheat him. But be warned, no one can cheat Death for ever.

Universe evolution.

Universe evolution. *you·knee·verse··ee·vo·loo·shon* – when the space containing everything that exists keeps changing, sometimes for better, sometimes for worse.

Congratulations on choosing Universe 1.0. Please follow the instructions correctly and we hope it will give you billions of years of trouble-free pleasure. It is a wonder that the Universe even exists in the first place. How on Earth did it get off the drawing board? You'd have to be mad to approve a self-expanding, all-encompassing void that contains everything, everyone and anything that has ever and will ever exist. What measurements were used? How big would the garden be? And due to the constant uncontrolled explosions, design, redesign, demolition and unparalleled turmoil, the nearby residents would be at the end of their tethers and the neighbourhood watch would be suicidal. But since the chicken[1] came before the egg,[2] the Universe continues to evolve. These revisions come at the expense of life forms, planets, galaxies and solar systems. Nothing is sacred, everything is expendable.

We're lucky that the Earth is even here for us to evolve on in the first place, especially as it seems that we might not feature in the Universe's final design – the Universe may want us dead. We've been pencilled in for annihilation at some point in the future, although we may kill ourselves long before the Universe has a chance to. Whatever happens, the human race is almost run.

WHEN WILL IT HAPPEN?	**WHEN SHOULD I START TO PANIC?**	**POSSIBILITY IT WILL HAPPEN?**
It's continually evolving as there's always room for improvement.	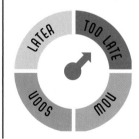	100%. The Universe is always on the move.
WHAT SHOULD I LOOK FOR?		**WHAT SHOULD I DO NEXT?**
Altered plans for the Universe in your local planning office.		Second guess how the Universe is going to end and try to figure out a sensible solution.

1. The Universe • 2. Planning regulations

Facsimile for the proposal of a new type of universe

(01) Planning Application (02) **PN1** (03) **0 000 001** (04) **A**

(05) Date of publication: **N/A**

(06) Application No: **0 000 001**

(07) Date of Filing: **N/A**

(08) Priority Data: **06543373**

(09) **UNIVERSAL TERRITORIES**

(10) INT CL: **HSZ 3/01020/04**

(11) Edition: **SBJ GHA002 F456 K327**

(12) Documents cited: **N1 4 33 45 7**

(13) Field of Search:
HSZ SDR 234 756 4 PRE

(14) Applicant(s): **GOD**

(15) Inventor(s): **GOD**

(16) Address: **HEAVEN**

(17) Abstract Title: **Universe**

(18) Brief Description:
The Universe will comprise a varying number of galaxies, which in turn will contain complex solar systems of stars and planets. (The total number of galaxies will not be determined until the universe planning permission has been granted.)

The Universe will be born out of every known element,[1] which have been combined in various quantities and compressed with the belief that a nuclear chain reaction will occur.

The resulting star dust and detritus will, over time, evolve into a system of complex life without any external influences.

(20) Drawing:
Fig 1: The early Universal model

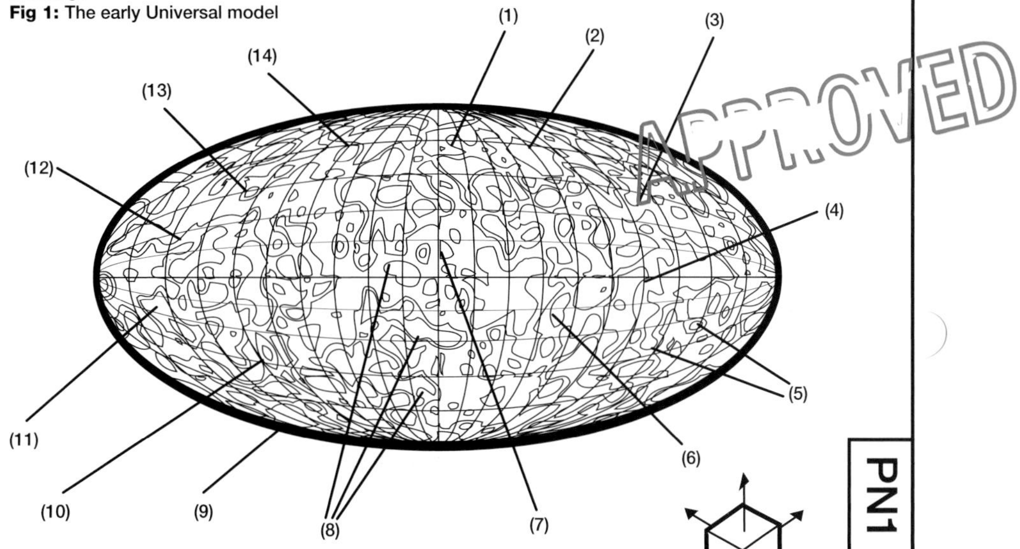

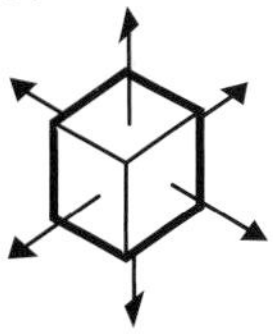

APPROVED

(21) Drawing:
Fig 2: Direction of universe expansion

PN1 0 000 001 A

[1] List of elements needed for universe production: **Actinium, Aluminium, Americium, Antimony, Argon, Arsenic, Astatine, Barium, Berkelium, Beryllium, Bismuth, Bohrium, Boron, Bromine, Cadmium, Calcium, Californium, Carbon, Cerium, Cesium, Chlorine, Chromium, Cobalt, Copper, Curium, Darmstadtium, Dubnium, Dysprosium, Einsteinium, Erbium, Europium, Fermium, Fluorine, Francium, Gadolinium, Gallium, Germanium, Gold, Hafnium, Hassium, Helium, Holmium, Hydrogen, Indium, Iodine, Iridium, Iron, Krypton, Lanthanum, Lawrencium, Lead, Lithium, Lutetium, Magnesium, Manganese, Meitnerium, Mendelevium, Mercury, Molybdenum, Neodymium, Neon, Neptunium, Nickel, Niobium, Nitrogen, Nobelium, Osmium, Oxygen, Palladium, Phosphorus, Platinum, Plutonium, Polonium, Potassium, Praseodymium, Promethium, Protactinium, Radium, Radon, Rhenium, Rhodium, Rubidium, Ruthenium, Rutherfordium, Samarium, Scandium, Seaborgium, Selenium, Silicon, Silver, Sodium, Strontium, Sulfur, Tantalum, Technetium, Tellurium, Terbium, Thallium, Thorium, Thulium, Tin, Titanium, Tungsten, Ununbium, Unununilium, Ununumium, Uranium, Vanadium, Xenon, Ytterbium, Yttrium, Zinc, Zirconium**

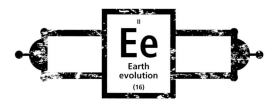

Ee

Earth evolution

(16)

Earth evolution. *errf·ee·vo·loo·shon* – from the sinking mud under your feet to the growing mountains that spoil your view, the Earth is the only home you will ever know, roll with the changes.

Our Earth has experienced a lot of growing pains since its birth, as it evolved from a tiny rocky nugget to the impressive green and blue ball we inhabit. In its infancy, the Earth was used as target practice by any passing space debris that fancied a bit of bullying. Over time, its weight and mass grew, as did its gravity, which in turn acted like a magnet to anything else that happened to be passing by. After growing to proportions similar to the size we see today, the Earth suffered a full-frontal attack by a Mars-sized planet called Theia. This collision resulted in the destruction of the attacker, but also in the creation of our bright and shiny moon. By overcoming its assailant the Earth proved it was capable of surviving anything that was thrown at it. And, so far, it has.

After a difficult childhood, a yet more troubled puberty set in. Earth's surface was ravaged by unsightly eruptions, tectonic activity and erosion. Earth needed parental guidance and who better to provide nurture than Mother Nature? From here on in, Earth flourished. Mother Nature has done a wonderful job but, even with her intervention, the ground underneath your feet remains troubled and there is no guarantee that Earth is going to continue to behave itself.

WHEN WILL IT HAPPEN?	**WHEN SHOULD I START TO PANIC?**	**WHAT SHOULD I DO NEXT?**
Now. It's changing all the time – it's just a little on the slow side.		We have to live with it. By using her natural erasers, including tsunamis, earthquakes, hurricanes and lava, Mother Nature tries to wipe us off the face of the Earth. But she can't erase us that easily ...
WHAT SHOULD I LOOK FOR?		
Volcanoes. When you see one erupting, think of it as a growth spurt.		

Facsimile for the proposal of a life-sustaining planet and its inhabitants

(01) Planning Application (02) **PN3** (03) **0 025 693** (04) **A**

(05) Date of publication: **N/A**

(06) Application No: **0 025 693**

(07) Date of Filing: **N/A**

(08) Priority Data: **06574856**

(09) **WORLD TERRITORIES**

(10) INT CL: **HSZ 3/01020/04**

(11) Edition: **SBJ GHA002 F456 K327**

(12) Documents cited: **BJ7 4555/99**

(13) Field of Search:
NONE

(14) Applicant(s): **GOD**

(15) Inventor(s): **GOD**

(16) Address: **HEAVEN**

(17) Abstract Title: **Life-sustaining planet Earth**

(18) Brief Description:
I plan to create a life-sustaining planet including all its inhabitants. I believe this can be achieved within a time frame of 7 (seven) days. I also seek planning permission to extend my residence of Heaven in the first day. The structure of my week includes:

Day 1: Heaven, Earth, Time, Water and Light

Day 2: Sky, broken down into various atmospheric levels

Day 3: Land, plants, trees

Day 4: Sun, moon, stars

Day 5: Creatures (Sea based), birds

Day 6: Creatures (Land based), Man (in my likeness)

Day 7: If all goes well, I may take the seventh day off

I think it will be good.

(20.1) Day 1a. Drawing:
i: Heaven and **ii** extension

(20.2) Day 1b. Drawing:
i: Earth, **ii:** Time, **iii:** Water, **iv:** Light

(20.3) Day 2. Drawing:
i: Sky

(20.4) Day 3. Drawing:
i: Land, **ii:** Plants, **iii:** Trees

(20.5) Day 4. Drawing:
i: Sun, **ii:** Moon, **iii:** Stars

(20.6) Day 5. Drawing:
i: Creatures (Sea based), **ii:** Birds

(20.7) Day 6. Drawing:
i: Creatures (Land based) **ii:** Man

fig. 20.5 i

fig. 20.2 i

fig. 20.4 i

fig. 20.5 iii

fig. 20.5 ii

REJECTED

REASON FOR REJECTION: Although the idea of creating a life-sustaining planet is a good, well thought-out idea, we believe that the time scale is unworkable. To create a fully working planet of this kind we feel that a more realistic time scale of approximately 4.6 billion years may be needed.

PN3 0 025 693 A

Uh
II
Universal
history
(18)

Important events in the history of the Universe to date. Each coloured dot represents a significant event. Each grey/black dot is equivalent to 1/10 of a billion years.

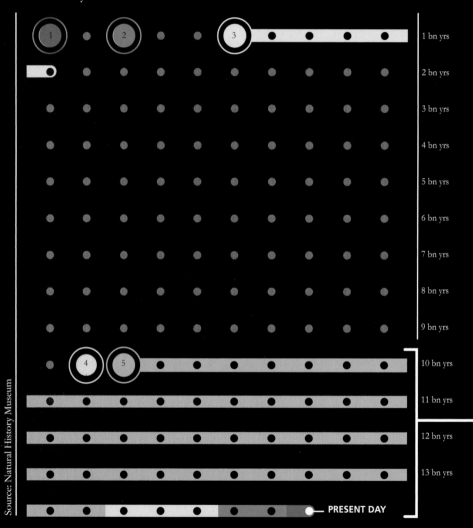

Source: Natural History Museum

1 bn yrs
2 bn yrs
3 bn yrs
4 bn yrs
5 bn yrs
6 bn yrs
7 bn yrs
8 bn yrs
9 bn yrs
10 bn yrs
11 bn yrs
12 bn yrs
13 bn yrs

PRESENT DAY

● The Big Bang ● Atoms form ● Gravity forms galaxies ● The Sun ignites/Solar system forms/ Earth's history begins ● Theia collides with Earth and the Moon is formed ● Present day ●&○ Everything else in between

Eh II
Earth history
(19)

Geological timeline of the Earth.

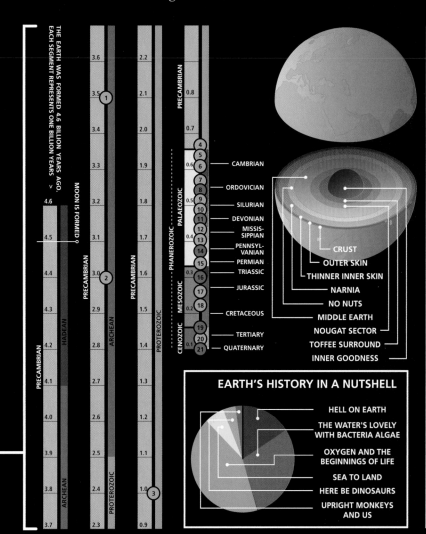

THE EARTH WAS FORMED 4.6 BILLION YEARS AGO.
EACH SEGMENT REPRESENTS ONE BILLION YEARS

MOON IS FORMED

4.6
4.5
4.4
4.3
4.2
4.1
4.0
3.9
3.8
3.7

HADEAN
ARCHEAN
PRECAMBRIAN

3.6
3.5
3.4
3.3
3.2
3.1
3.0
2.9
2.8
2.7
2.6
2.5
2.4
2.3

ARCHEAN
PROTEROZOIC
PRECAMBRIAN

2.2
2.1
2.0
1.9
1.8
1.7
1.6
1.5
1.4
1.3
1.2
1.1
1.0
0.9

PROTEROZOIC
PRECAMBRIAN

0.8
0.7
0.6
0.5
0.4
0.3
0.2
0.1

PRECAMBRIAN
PHANEROZOIC
PALAEOZOIC
MESOZOIC
CENOZOIC

CAMBRIAN
ORDOVICIAN
SILURIAN
DEVONIAN
MISSIS-SIPPIAN
PENNSYL-VANIAN
PERMIAN
TRIASSIC
JURASSIC
CRETACEOUS
TERTIARY
QUATERNARY

CRUST
OUTER SKIN
THINNER INNER SKIN
NARNIA
NO NUTS
MIDDLE EARTH
NOUGAT SECTOR
TOFFEE SURROUND
INNER GOODNESS

Extinction and Life time line source: Natural History Museum

EARTH'S HISTORY IN A NUTSHELL

HELL ON EARTH

THE WATER'S LOVELY WITH BACTERIA ALGAE

OXYGEN AND THE BEGINNINGS OF LIFE

SEA TO LAND

HERE BE DINOSAURS

UPRIGHT MONKEYS AND US

● Early Microfossils discovered (3.5 bya) ● Cyanobacteria form oxygen (3.0 bya) ● Simple cells (1.0 bya) ● Multicellular animals (570 mya) ● Shells/Skeletons (545 mya) ● Fish (500 mya) ● Land plants (455 mya) ● End-Ordovician-Silurian extinction (443 mya) ● Land dwelling arthropods/Sharks/Wingless Insects (420/410/400 mya) ● Trees/Amphibian & reptile ancestors (390/375 mya) ● Late-Devonian extinction (370 mya) ● Amphibians/Flying Insects (325/340 mya) ● Reptiles (300 mya) ● End-Permian-Triassic extinction (248 mya) ● Dinosaurs/Mammals (235/230 mya) ● Late-Triassic extinction (210 mya) ● Birds (145 mya) ● Flowering plants (130 mya) ● Cretaceous-Tertiary extinction (65 mya) ● Primates/Great apes (54 mya/25 mya) ● Present-day extinctions due to human activity

Water. *war-tar* – **the clear liquid essential for all living things. We can drink it and swim, sail or drown in it, but without it we couldn't have evolved.**

Water is your transparent best friend. You wouldn't be here without it. It's been your best friend since the very beginning, long before you were even a glint in a Prokaryotic[1] eye. Without water, the Prokaryotic wouldn't have evolved into a creature that could grow eyes, that's how good a friend water has been to us and every other living thing that existed. So let us raise a glass of water and drink to water, your transparent best friend.

  Water had other friends too before you came along: Earth, Wind and Fire. They'd been together from the very beginning but a falling-out led to Water going solo, whereas Earth, Wind and Fire went on to have a string of hits.[2] This highlights the fickleness of water, due to the various states it gets itself into. We all know that water comes in solid, liquid or vapour form. These three states can be further split into two sub-categories: *Aqua Contentus* and *Aqua Aestuosus*. What category of water do you have coming from your taps? *Aqua Contentus* is often described as the happy side of water. A calm ocean can be referred to as a *blissful sea*, the frozen water in your freezer is also known as *delighted water,* whereas a newly boiled kettle emits *happy precipitation (or gay vapour)*, not forgetting fresh snow, or *pleasure frost*. But with the good inevitably comes the bad and like all your human best friends, water is not always in a happy state.

WHAT SHOULD I LOOK FOR?	WHEN SHOULD I START TO PANIC?	WHAT SHOULD I DO NEXT?
Water can be deceptive. whether it be in the seas, the rivers, the lakes or even in the air, it can turn angry pretty quickly. Be aware of all its states and recognise the symptoms before it's too late.		Batten down the hatches. With climate change kicking in, the watery weather is due to go schizo on your ass. Expect more floods, larger cyclonic storms and seas rising up to engulf you.

1. A Prokaryotic is a very basic creature that doesn't have eyes • 2. The *Last Days and Time* album is by far the best

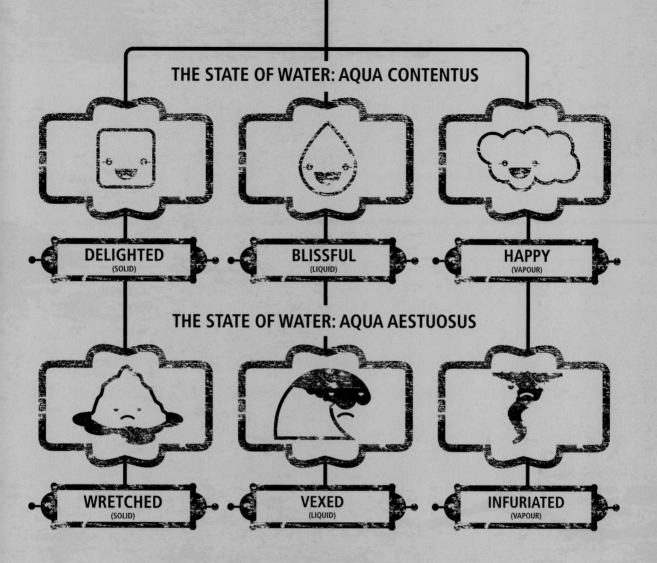

THE STATE OF WATER: AQUA CONTENTUS

DELIGHTED
(SOLID)

BLISSFUL
(LIQUID)

HAPPY
(VAPOUR)

THE STATE OF WATER: AQUA AESTUOSUS

WRETCHED
(SOLID)

VEXED
(LIQUID)

INFURIATED
(VAPOUR)

Aqua Aestuosus or *agitated water* deals with the unhappy side of water. Unhappy water can manifest itself in various forms, from slightly unseasonal tides to enormous tsunamis and hurricanes.

A large mass of frozen water is *wretched ice*; waves and tsunamis fall into the category of *vexed water* and cyclonic events are categorised as *infuriated precipitation*. But for now let's celebrate the existence of happy water while we can. Just don't make him angry, you wouldn't like it when he's angry …

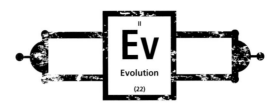

Ev
Evolution
(22)

Evolution. *ee·vo·loo·shon* – a series of upgrades in the development of a living organism. Each change being 'better' than the previous one.[1]

Human evolution has come a long way since its watery beginnings. Our journey has been a rollercoaster ride known as *The Evolution Revolution*. A ride of ascents and dips, acceleration and braking, inversions and separations, all starting with simple organic molecules in the waters of an early Earth. These single-celled ancestors were so revolutionary that they stayed happily single and unattached for the next billion years.

WHEN WILL IT HAPPEN?

Come back in a few million years' time and look at what we've become. Our human design is constantly under review.

WHAT SHOULD I LOOK FOR?

An increase or decrease in intellect, unusual eating habits, corrupted language and basic word skills, extra body parts or accelerated monsterism. (Do you know this type of person? Check out your local teenagers.)

WHEN SHOULD I START TO PANIC?

The upgrade, Homonid 10.9, is already being worked on. The changes won't be obvious for many years to come.

POSSIBILITY IT WILL HAPPEN?

100%. The evolution revolution is continual.

WHAT SHOULD I DO NEXT?

Once you have grown your new evolutionary features, figure out how to use them to maximum effect.

You'll need to decide whether to use your new-found limbs or super abilities for good or evil.

If you gain the power of X-ray vision, you can use this new found skill for good, whereas if you've grown enormous tentacles, use them for evil; they'll be perfect to assist your evil deeds.

---

1. Please note: modifications may not be obvious to the naked eye • 2. This half-reptile, half-mammal, plant-eating brute named Lystrosaurus survived the Permian-Triassic mass extinction event that wiped

Eventually craving company, they divided and became multicellular. From this moment there was no stopping them. They became complex, reproductive, cartilaginously flexible, organismistic, primitive, spiracled, skeletal, skulled, flippered, scaled, armoured, predatory, respiratory, legged, land-lubbered, mobile, adaptable, reptilian, barrel-chested, widespread, herbivorous, cow-sized and very very lucky.

By this stage our ancestors had evolved into one ugly-looking and damn lucky brute that survived the PT mass extinction event.[2] Virtually overnight, give or take a few hundred years, this beastie became the dominant and most widespread

EXIT

creature on the planet and stayed that way for millions of years.

With all this time at our disposal we regenerated and became mammalian, warm-blooded, parental, furry, smaller, burrowing, oppressed, and nocturnal, so by the time the dinosaurs were in charge, we were usefully small and kept well out of their way for millions of years.

As dinosaurs ruled the Earth, we watched as a handily timed asteroid brought about their extinction. From here on we became cerebral, ape-like, erect, aware, communicative, inventive, hunters, gatherers, farmers, spiritual and social, resulting in the varied collection of humans you see around you every day.[3] So with this much evolution under our belts, what's next? Well, the power of flight and night vision would be nice but, unfortunately, becoming super human isn't part of the plan. The indications are that we could split off into two human sub-species. One group would be fit and athletic, healthy and tall, the other would be short, overweight, unhealthy couch potatoes. So forget the survival of the fittest, they'll be fine, it's the survival of the fattest we've got to worry about.[4]

out around 95% of *all* life on Earth • 3. Please note: list of evolutionary traits may not be in this order
4. *See* Obesity (138)

III

Biblically stressed

Biblically stressed. *bib·lick·alley··stair·rest* – featured in a religious book that explains the origins of life, the Universe and everything.[1]

*** WARNING: BIBLE SPOILER ALERT ***

The book that gave us the 'Armageddon' word predicts the ultimate demise of the human race. The Bible is an epic tale of sex and incest, love and war, flood and famine, jealousy and murder. It follows a father and son's[2] journey through the entire 6,000 years of Earth's history.[3] With the success of the first book, a well-received second volume followed and became even more successful than the original, even though it ends on a cliffhanger. Followers of the religious text believe it predicts the ultimate end of humankind so maybe it's time to start praying for your soul.

---

1. Please note: other explanations are available • 2. The twist is that the father *is* the father *and* the son *and* the holy ghost all at the same time • 3. Some say the Earth is 6,000 years old, others say 4.6 billion, give or take a few years ...

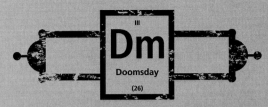

III

Dm

Doomsday

(26)

Doomsday. *dooms·day* – Armageddon, the apocalypse, the end of days. Whatever you want to call it, it's the end of the world as we know it.

All good things must come to an end and in the case of Doomsday, life as we know it will come to an end after an enormous showdown.

The Bible predicts that at the end of days there is to be one almighty rumble in the jungle between the two giants of religion: one on the side of good and the other fighting for evil. In the good corner we have the all-powerful, undisputed king of the Universe, your lord and master, God. And in the evil corner we have the challenger – the fallen angel, the prince of darkness, he who puts the romance in necromancer, Old Nick himself, the one and only, Satan.

The Bible observes that the final outcome of this epic fight falls in God

WHEN WILL IT HAPPEN?

Soon, start praying ...

WHAT SHOULD I LOOK FOR?

A big white guy and a big red guy fighting. Dark and thunderous skies that form quickly out of nowhere.

Unconventional weapons may be used, including thunderbolts and lightning, and elements such as the wind and fire. Earthquakes may be felt.

Also the resurrection of the dead may occur.

WHEN SHOULD I START TO PANIC?

For the religious Doomsday believers, it's not a matter of 'if', but 'when'. It doesn't have to start with a God vs. Satan rumble. If an asteroid strikes, a supervolcano erupts or a mega tsunami hits, it can all be put down to God's wrath.

WHAT SHOULD I DO NEXT?

It's Judgment Day and we're all going to be judged for our heinous crimes. What dark secrets do you have hidden in your murky past that make you squirm?

Do you think you're worthy enough to climb the stairway to Heaven? If not then you'd better start righting all those horrible wrongs that you've committed.

If you've ever killed someone, you've got a hell of a lot of do-gooding to do.

and his followers' favour. So if you're not part of God's gang prepare for Hell on Earth while God and his followers take the stairway to Heaven to party in the clouds for all eternity. The fight between good and evil will see Satan waging war on God (and his followers) to ultimately overthrow Him and take His throne. The smart money would be on God to win, but if He's having an off day then be prepared for a very unhappy eternity.

So maybe it's time to start believing or gatecrash the party – free drinks and all you can eat for ever and ever – Amen.

Satan. *say·ton* – difficult to spot as a positive identification has yet to be made. He may have horns and cloven feet or he may look just like me or you. Landlord of Hell, his long-term lodgers include Pol Pot and Hitler. He's already set aside the spare room for current evil-doers.[1]

We've been warned that he's coming for thousands of years. It has been hailed as the beginning of the end of the human race as we know it.

We've been kept abreast of his mischief by numerous prophets of doom throughout history, but as yet, we're still here and, hopefully, he's still down there. If Satan does succeed in his attempts to overthrow God, then Hell will be moved up from the dusty basement and ensconced on Earth's ground floor. Life is going to get hard. Your day will start with compulsory chain carrying followed by sleep deprivation, abuse and

WHAT SHOULD I LOOK FOR?

We've had many false alarms but Satan can be spotted. Although he is a master of disguise he can be caught out. Catch him without his flesh-coloured make-up and he's mainly red in hue. Look out for oversized hounds with bright red eyes, evil children with spinning heads and spouting foul obscenities.

Hairdressers should search the scalps of customers just in case the mark of the Devil[2] is hiding under the hair.

WHEN SHOULD I START TO PANIC?

Difficult to say. The end is nigher depending on how religious you are.

Non-believers can rest easy while some believe Satan is due to call on us very soon. Some say he's already here. Is your neighbour the Devil? Are you he?

POSSIBILITY IT WILL HAPPEN?

NON-RELIGIOUS   RELIGIOUS

OLD NICK-NAMES

Satan, Old Nick, the Devil, the Antichrist, Beelzebub, the Prince of Darkness, Lucifer, Abaddon or El Diablo amongst others – may be too conspicuous. He may choose a common name such as Colin or Shirley – any name could be used. Listen out for names like 'Louis Cypher'.

---

1. They say you can judge a person by the company he keeps ... • 2. 666 is the number of the beastie
3. ... or deathtime

torture. The dormant evil inside us all will be massaged and weedled out, so we can become part of a vast evil army against good God.

If the Devil does rise up, our fight against global warming will have been futile. As soon as the Devil moves in then the heat will be turned up to eleven and the ice caps will be gone before you can say: *Burn in Hell*.

With the destruction of life as you know it going on all around you, you'd think that death would be a welcome relief, but dying under the reign of Satan would guarantee you a lifetime[3] of torture in the vats of Hell. Your only option is to stick it out until God's come-back tour.

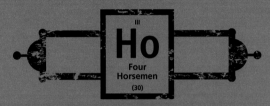

III
Ho
Four Horsemen
(30)

Four Horsemen. *for·whores·men* – four pissed-off jockeys from Hell on a mission to destroy you and everything you know.

Planning an uprising against the very deity that designed you, the Universe and everything in it would be pretty foolhardy. The odds are slimmer than a skeleton at fat camp but that is exactly what Satan's planning. But even for a smart cookie such as Satan, the battle is lost long before he can put on his lucky socks as:

• It's predicted that he'll lose, it says so in the Book of Revelation
• God is omnipresent – He can read Satan's thoughts and battle plans before he's formed them in his big red head.

The good news for Satan is that he'll have a kick-ass army behind him. It has also been foreseen in the Bible that his army will be headed up by four

WHEN WILL IT HAPPEN?

The Four Horsemen of the Apocalypse will begin their murderous spree across Earth soon after dawn on Doomsday. Like Satanic Santas they'll try to purge Earth in a day. Make sure you're out when they come calling, and block the chimney.

WHAT SHOULD I LOOK FOR?

A door opening in the sky and all hell breaking loose. Beware of anyone, or thing, on horseback.

WHEN SHOULD I START TO PANIC?

RATE YOUR MORAL COMPASS

WHAT SHOULD I DO NEXT?

Learn a useful martial art such as black tiger kung fu, ju-jitsu or Egyptian stick fencing. Combine these skills with riding horseback and you may have a chance in single combat with Conquest, War, and possibly Famine. Steer clear of Death at all costs.

Either that or take an interest in religion. Hopefully by the time The Big Bad Four arrive you'll already be in the departure line for the stairway to Heaven.

---

1. Always up for a challenge • 2. Loves a good fight, fair or unfair • 3. The only warrior who can fight on an empty stomach • 4. Satan in disguise

Come and have a go if you think you're hard enough.

equestrian-savvy warriors, Conquest,[1] War,[2] Famine[3] and Death.[4]

With this quartet on his side, how can Satan possibly lose? Should he really trust a team that has been handed to him on a plate by God's own book? Has God forced Satan to pick the team He wanted him to choose. Is it a devilishly cunning double bluff? Is Famine a double agent, bribed with the promise of an All You Can Eat buffet at the outcome?

We'll find out the answers when Doomsday finally arrives. Satan's death squad is going to try to heap misery on our sorry asses and God help us if he wins. When the Four Horsemen start a reapin', you'd better start a weepin'.

Aps
Apocalysmo
III
(32)

Cut out the Four Horsemen of the Apocalypse provided and choose which horseman you would like to be from Conquest (1), War (2), Famine (3) and Death (4). Cut out and assemble the die at the back of the book (259). Place all the Horsemen in the Paddocks of Hell. Each player should roll the die once; the player with the highest score goes first.

Move the amount of squares shown on the die. If you land on a square with an instruction, do as instructed.

The winner is the first player to reach Earth on square 74. The winner's prize is a chance to destroy the entire world. Start by destroying your own bedroom and everything in it, move on to the rest of the house and garage contents, cause havoc in your community then take on the rest of the world on a rampage of death and destruction. Cause as much mayhem as you can before you get arrested.

Good luck!

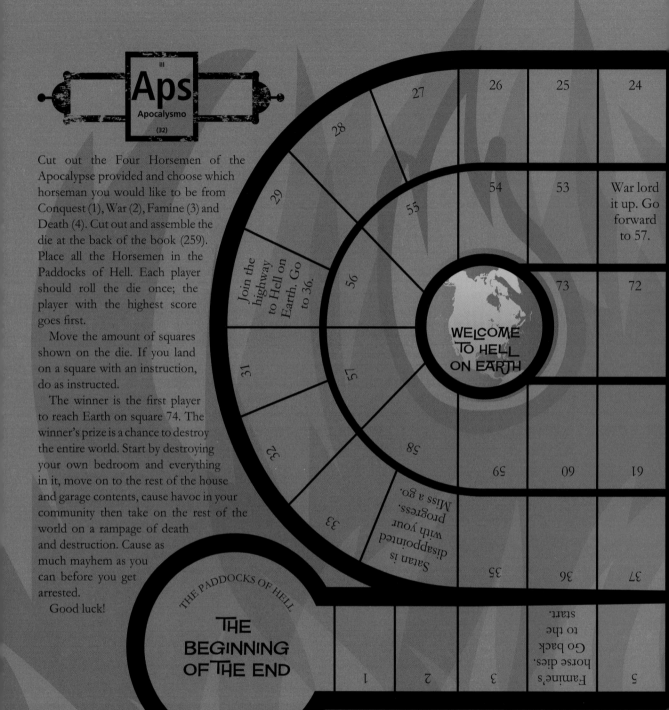

THE PADDOCKS OF HELL

THE BEGINNING OF THE END

WELCOME TO HELL ON EARTH

27 28 29 31 32 33 35 36 37 5 3 2 1

24 25 26 54 53 War lord it up. Go forward to 57.

73 72 55 56 51 57 58 59 60 61

Join the highway to Hell on Earth. Go to 36.

Satan is disappointed with your progress. Miss a go.

Famine's horse dies. Go back to the start.

22 | 21 | You can't cheat Death. Go back to 10. | 19 | 18 | 17 | 16 | 15 | 14 | 13 | 12

50 | 49 | 48 | 47 | 46 | 45

70 | Conqest has a confidence crisis. Go back to 60. | 68 | 67 | 66 | 65

The end is nigh. Fast forward to 66. | 64

Famine stops to eat. Miss a go.

43 | 42 | 41 | 40 | 39

11 | 10 | 6 | 8 | 7

I

2

3

4

III

Fl

Flood

(34)

Flood. *flud* – **when excess water leaves the rivers and lakes and seeks refuge in your towns, schools and hallway.**

The only thing worse than a vengeful God is a fickle one. The Great Flood that wiped out everyone and everything that hadn't pre-booked a place on Noah's zoo cruise was sent by a God who felt His creation was not going exactly the way He'd planned. Retribution was easier than rehabilitation.

And just like God, you can't reason with the weather. Too little rain and you have a drought, too much rain and you've got yourself a great big floody hell.

With the unpredictable weather that climate change is set to bring plus the anger of a vengeful creator, you should start thinking about trading in your motorcar for a motorboat.

WHEN WILL IT HAPPEN?

A great flood starts with a single raindrop so be wary every time you feel rain on your skin. Always have an umbrella and a dinghy in tow and enough food for 40 days and nights.

WHAT SHOULD I LOOK FOR?

Nasty-looking clouds. A wall of water heading towards you all at once.

Your ground floor being turned into a swimming pool in seconds and kippers in your slippers.

WHEN SHOULD I START TO PANIC?

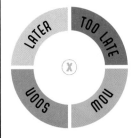

To determine when you need to panic, answer the following questions:

Do you live near water?
Do you live on a hill?
Can you swim?
Are you a sinner?

How did you rate?
Yes x 1 – Later • Yes x 2 – Soon
Yes x 3 – Now • Yes x 4 – Too late

WHERE NOT TO LIVE

The Netherlands, as nearly all of the country is below sea level. People living in low-lying places are under threat from rising sea levels.

Also Amsterdam, New York, New Orleans, London, the Amazon Basin, Venice and St Petersburg, amongst many many others.

WHAT SHOULD I DO NEXT?

Learn to swim or live on a boat.

Dr

III

Drought

(36)

Drought. *der·rout* – when the rain refuses to fall and the world's land becomes as dry as a sandstorm on a sunbed.

God's wrath has been well documented up to 2,000 years ago when records of God's anger management stops. God took his frustrations out on man with catastrophic events that caused untold hardship.

Angering a vengeful God with a huge arsenal of suffering at his disposal is not a smart move, but since the end of God's documented anger issues, we've learnt that it doesn't always take an angry deity to cause a drought. The world is hotting up, which makes crops fail and causes the land to become drier than the inside of a skeleton's airing cupboard. Lakes and reservoirs are rapidly evaporating and water shortages becoming increasingly common.

Within the century, Perth is due to become the world's first ghost city, as it drinks the last stocks of its underwater reservoir dry, resulting in it being abandoned; Spain has been importing water from France, and if the glaciers in the Himalayas melt then India, Nepal and the other surrounding countries will be hit first with icy floods and then with a very long and hot drought.

WHEN WILL IT HAPPEN?

When it hasn't rained for a long long time.

WHAT SHOULD I LOOK FOR?

Day after day of relentless burning sunshine and clear blue skies, withered plants and sad-looking crops. It's about this time you should pray for rain.

WHEN SHOULD I START TO PANIC?

The world's lakes, glaciers, oceans and reservoirs are making a break for it.

WHAT SHOULD I DO NEXT?

Preserve water. Invent a device to collect melt water from Greenland's glaciers before it has a chance to take a dip in the salty sea and becomes undrinkable.

Then there really will be water, water everywhere and not a freshwater drop to drink.

III

Fa

Famine

(38)

Famine. *fam·in* – when hunger comes a-knocking on everyone's door a few weeks before Death comes to stay.

The last two millennia have been littered with famine, from grain famines in ancient Rome to diseased potatoes in Ireland and more besides. You may think that modern-day famines are restricted to Africa, but all it takes is an unforeseen event and we'll all go hungry, no matter which continent we live in. A famine can be caused by factors such as insects, disease, drought and political unrest, amongst many others. In our modern world, foods such as rice or bananas are clocking up more air miles than a pigeon with a pilot's licence, so disrupt the food supply chain and you've got a lot of hungry people on your hands.

Food shortages and ultimately famine could occur if there is any sort of catastrophic crop-destroying event, or food chain supply collapse. Add escalating food and fuel prices into the mix and countries relying on aid will suffer first, followed by the rest of us turning our local parks and green spaces into allotments. In the event of a worldwide famine, various open spaces throughout the world have been earmarked for the cultivation of crops. London's Green Park is one example, it will be used to grow only green vegetables, except for peas, as they will be grown in Peace parks.

WHEN WILL IT HAPPEN?	**WHEN SHOULD I START TO PANIC?**	**WHAT SHOULD I LOOK FOR?**
Almost all societies, rich and poor, have suffered from famine in the past; it can happen when you least expect it. With the planet warming up and the schizo world economy in free fall anything is possible: never take another meal for granted ever again.	 Stock up on bottled water, UHT milk, cream crackers and rice.	Insect invasion, fire, disease, too much or too little sun, too much or too little rain, loss of biodiversity, damaged ecosystem, desertification, erosion, political or social unrest, unemployment or power loss ... these are just some of the things to make you hungry.

III
PI
Plague and pestilence
(40)

Plague and pestilence. *playg··and··pes·till·ants* – a swath of disease laying waste to land creatures or a swarm of creatures laying waste to the land.

In biblical times a plague was one of the preferred vengeance tools of God to destroy all non-believers or just to get his own way with an 'I told you so' on a biblical scale.

An angered God can turn your days into night at the drop of a hat. He can rain down a storm of locusts, flies, gnats, frogs and hail on your unworthy ass, and, if that wasn't enough, he can kill you and the rest of your livestock, turn your rivers to blood, kill your first-born and cover your body in hideous sores until you get the message. If only modern-day plagues were this discriminating.

In current times we're still under threat from some of these ancient plagues: locusts periodically take flight and eat anything and everything in sight, Bubonic plague is still an underlying threat, even though we've got the antibiotics to deal with it, and fly spray will sort out the annoying flies. So if there is another shitstorm coming our way from God, let's hope He just sends the frogs[1]: at least they'll eat the gnats.

WHAT SHOULD I LOOK FOR?	WHEN SHOULD I START TO PANIC?	WHAT SHOULD I DO NEXT?
The skies turning black with flying creatures. Red water flowing from the taps. Amphibians reclaiming the streets.	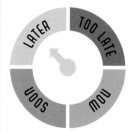	Remove the insects or amphibians from your house, bath, hair, eyes, dinner, mouth, nose, car, bed, pants, lunchbox. Pavements will be knee deep in insect carcasses, a clean-up operation will need to ensue. Everyone should help, except for any first-borns ...
LOCUST WEATHER REPORT		
The dreaded swarms will form in years of heavy rain with a period of good harvests.	When you hear the angry voice of God and the sky goes dark.	

1. A plague of frogs occurs when a waterspout travels across a garden pond and picks up the creature with his extended family eventually re-housing them thousands of miles away

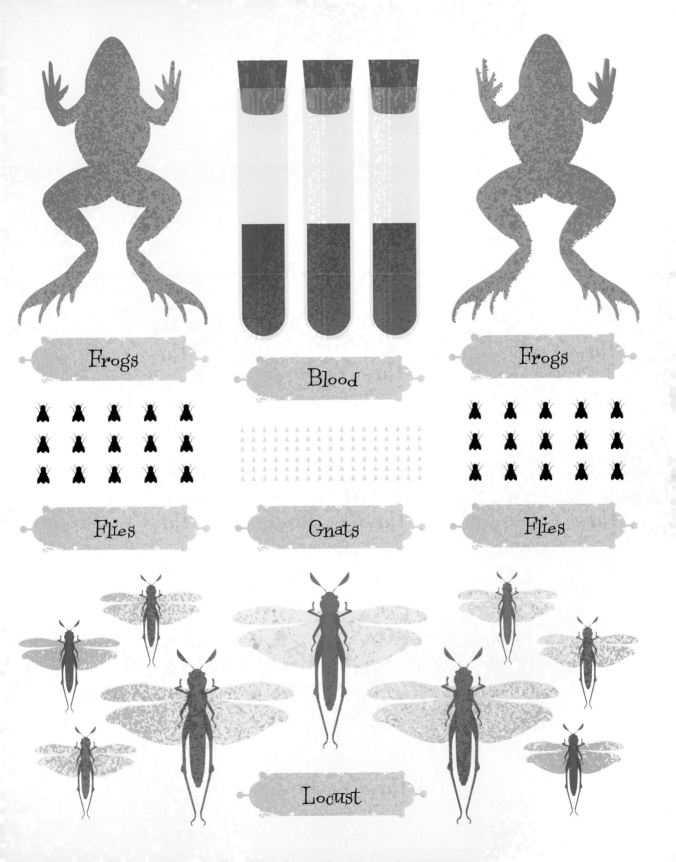

Frogs

Blood

Frogs

Flies

Gnats

Flies

Locust

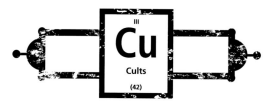

Cults

Cults. *kults* – followers of an extreme devotion with a religious or non-religious theme.

If you believe the end is nigh and nobody else believes you except for a few close friends, form a cult. But be careful, cults have got a bad name over the years, as it only takes a few rotten apples to taint the whole barrel. Since when have you heard a positive story about a cult on the news? In most cases you wouldn't know there was a cult living next door to you,[1] usually they keep themselves to themselves, patiently waiting for their own end, but some groups are not content with localised salvation, they want to bring the end to other people too, with murderous consequences. Some groups announce an end date, but if it looks like the end may not happen it leaves the group with only two options: a, pick a new date or b, save face and instigate the end themselves ... after all, once bitten, twice nigh.

WHEN WILL IT HAPPEN?

The end is always nigh for members of a cult – that's the reason that they've all assembled for the final gathering in the first place.

WHAT SHOULD I LOOK FOR?

A group of people with distant looks in their eyes who are dressed in exactly the same way and appear to be waiting for someone or something. Also look for a glowing growing light in the sky.

WHEN SHOULD I START TO PANIC?

If you've already joined ...

as for the rest of us ...

POSSIBILITY IT WILL HAPPEN?

When it comes to cults, we only realise the threat when it's too late so keep your eyes open, people.

It also depends if they're right and the rest of the entire world is wrong.[2]

CULT CLASSICS

If you're thinking of starting your own cult, popular cult subjects include: aliens, the second coming, Satan, the occult, *Star Trek* or all of the above.

---

1. Apart from the large amount of people entering the house with very few ever exiting again • 2. *See* Mayan calendar: 2012 (146)

CULT FOLLOWING

Members of the Yuthon Society are looking for new followers to join our gathering of like-minded individuals.

Yuthonism promotes our beliefs to the wider world through outspoken members and news grabbing headlines.

CULT REQUIREMENTS

To become a Yuthid, applicants must be able to:

* Follow the crowd *
* Carry out destructive orders *
* Be secretive *
* Shun their family *
* Move in with 50 other members *
* Take part in mass suicide (TBC) *

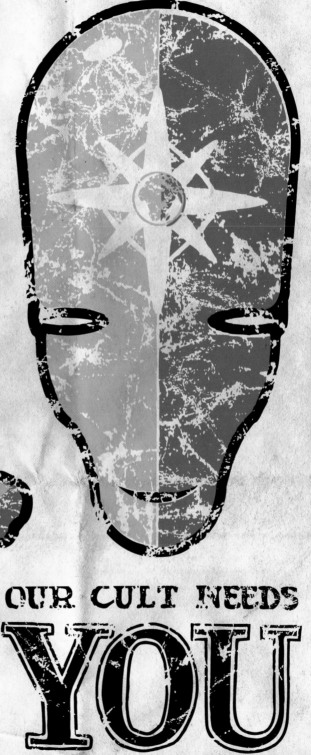

OUR CULT NEEDS

YOU

III
Rw
Religious warfare
(44)

Religious warfare. *re·lid·jus··warf·air* – when breaking two of the Ten Commandments becomes unavoidable.

With thousands of religions in the world and countless more gods, it's not surprising that, over the years, things have got a little intolerant down here on Earth. While we're fighting far below, up in the heavens, the gods of varying religions sit back on their clouds and watch their creations fight it out in their very own live version of a simulation game, but unfortunately for us, we don't get the option of the extra lives and power-ups. Loving thy neighbour and abstaining from killing are the first two commandments to bite the dust and the 'My god is better than your god' fighting will keep occurring until our God or gods[1] come out of hiding and reveal all. At this point, religious warfare will really kick off. Expect the believers of the newly revealed true faiths to get even more biblical on your ass.

WHEN WILL IT HAPPEN?

Religious warfare and intolerance have been around as long as religion itself.

Loving thy neighbour isn't easy when you've got feuding landlords with opposing points of view.

WHAT SHOULD I LOOK FOR?

Peace, love, harmony and religious tolerance throughout the world ... but if you can't find it then get ready for more intolerance with a side order of war.

WHEN SHOULD I START TO PANIC?

Religion is, literally, set in stone.[2] Trying to change someone's religious point of view can be a pointless exercise (unless you do it via brain-washing).[3]

WHICH RELIGION SHOULD I FOLLOW?

God knows ...

DEFRAGGED BEYOND BELIEF

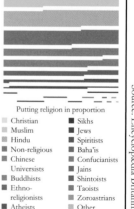

Putting religion in proportion

Christian	Sikhs
Muslim	Jews
Hindu	Spiritists
Non-religious	Baha'is
Chinese Universists	Confucianists
Buddhists	Jains
Ethno-religionists	Shintoists
Atheists	Taoists
Neoreligionists	Zoroastrians
	Other Religionists

Source: Encyclopædia Britannica

---

1. Delete where applicable • 2. *See* the Ten Commandments for further details • 3. *See* Cults (42)

Papal Scissors Stone

The only way to
solve religious conflict

The paper of God
The half prayer

The scissors of God
The blessing

The stone of God
The wrath

Paper
defeats **Stone**

Scissors
defeats **Paper**

Stone
defeats **Scissors**

IV
Acts of God

Acts of God. *akts··ov··god* – when it's not your fault, it's *his/her/their*[1] fault. **When God takes matters into His own hands.**

The rock that we live on is constantly reshaping, and if you're in the wrong place at the wrong time then you're in right trouble.

  The Earth is under constant upheaval, it's being ripped apart and rebuilt while man is washed away, engulfed, buried, burned and made homeless by unseen forces that our legal system, in our culture-of-blame society, has decided to lay at the invisible feet of the big man upstairs.[2] It's all God's fault ... within reason.[3]

  So while we wait for Doomsday to happen, keep one eye on the kids in your backyard and the other on the tornado on the horizon

---

1. Delete where applicable • 2. You don't even have to believe He exists to claim • 3. God is responsible for the howling winds in the air and in your ears, the angry water in the sea, the shaking ground under your feet and the explosive insides of the Earth coming out, the thunder, the lightning, all of which is very, very frightening. But unfortunately not the noisy neighbour who lives upstairs ...

IV
Act
Acts of God
(48)

Acts of God. *akts··ov··god* – when the wind and the rain, the Earth and the seas, and the fire that scorcheth the land can be blamed on an invisible man.

Take a look at your insurance policy and you'll see a clause referring to an 'Act of God'.[1] Whether you believe in a higher being or not, the clause is always there. When your car is swallowed up by a big hole in the ground that wasn't there before or your front room becomes a submarine overnight, you can thank the Lord for his legal forethought. (For further reading, *see* the facsimile of the Act of God Proclamation opposite.)

'Acts of God' refers to the unpredictable forces of nature that will rise up and try to crush you; to wash or whisk you away or to make you very wet and homeless indeed. One or a combination of these forces: wind, water, earth and fire is the usual suspect in one of God's 'acts'.

WHAT SHOULD I LOOK FOR?

Death and destruction that appears to be sent by an unseen and vengeful force from above. It may come in one or more of the following forms: flood, lake overturns, heavy rain, thunder, lightning, mudslides, landslides, wildfires earthquakes, tsunamis, avalanches, hurricanes, cyclones or volcanoes, amongst other events that want to wipe you off the face of the Earth and destroy all your stuff.

WHEN SHOULD I START TO PANIC?

It depends how the small print reads on your house or life insurance policies.

If disastrous natural acts cannot be blamed on a higher being then be prepared to dig deep into your very shallow pockets.

POSSIBILITY IT WILL HAPPEN?

Natural disasters are inevitable; you can't escape the Earth in turmoil but you can prepare for the worst. Build your house far inland to prevent the sea from rising up and engulfing your property. Add stilts to your house to avoid floods and mudslides. Avoid living at the base of mountains or volcanoes. Don't live somewhere too hot or cold; better yet, live in a mobile home and drive away from disaster.

1. Not to be confused with 'Act of Satan' clause or 'Santa Claus'

ACT OF GOD
PROCLAMATION

1 IN THE BEGINNING, God created the Heavens and the Earth and everything that has been and gone since the very beginning[a].

2 Once near completion, God gave the Earth top-end finishes and furnishings for the 'right kind of people' to inhabit his land.

3 The first tenants of Earth were named Adam and Eve, and for a time it was good.

4 They enjoyed the benefits of God's hard work: from the rivers to the mountains, from the beasts in the field to the trees in the garden.

5 But the good times were not to last, for God asked the tenants not to go near his beloved apple tree. The fruit of his labour was his and his alone. But to God's dismay, they ate the fruit.

6 For defying the Lord of the land[b] they were evicted, never to return.

7 From this day forth, God annulled the freedoms that humankind had enjoyed. He begat a team of legal eagles to draft an agreement that God may enjoy and man may endure. The legal eagles set to work.

8 Seven days and nights passed. On the morn of the eighth day, an 'Act of God' was laid bare for all to see.

9 The Act of God came to be, and was circulated throughout the land.

10 And humankind had to adhere to this agreement for evermore.

THE AGREEMENT

2 IT IS DECREED THAT: **You**[c] (hereinafter called 'MAN') and **the almighty God of the Heavens and the Earth** (hereinafter called 'GOD') will abide by the laws of this agreement.

1 This agreement is brought into effect from the day you were born.

2 No signature is required due to the omnipresence of God. He was present at your birth and knows who you are.

3 The agreement is binding, non-negotiable and watertight, between God and Man.

3 RIGHTS
The following rights are granted to God and God alone:

1 God may control the AIR in the skies. God has the right to huff and puff and blow your house down, without prior arrangement.

2 God may command the WATER from the seven seas or the rivers and the lakes or the rain in the sky and dispatch the moisture on to the land.

3 God may summon up FIRE and burn your shed down.

iv God may invoke the EARTH to shake without prior warning.

4 God may employ thunderbolts and lightning that may be very, very frightening.

4 DISPUTES
God is:

1 Happy to take the blame for natural disasters, but will not make any court appearances.

2 Not responsible for wars or disagreements that arise through the disputes of man with another man.

3 Not interested in disputes about his existence as he and he alone knows whether he exists or not.

4 Unpredictable. He may or may not be happy to help.

5 EXCEPTIONS
There are no exceptions as:

1 It is required that every man, woman and child will be bound by the decrees set out in this agreement, regardless of belief, race, age or sex.

2 A belief in the existence of God is necessary.

3 The 'Act of God' cannot be cancelled or modified.

4 A person that 'didn't ask to be born' is not exempt.

6 DESIRE
It is God's desire for you to know good and evil[d].

7 WARRANTIES
By entering into this agreement:

1 You will be bound by the terms and conditions set out.

2 God has removed your power to opt out of this agreement.

8 IN CONCLUSION
May the good winds blow for you and may it rain a thousand rains on your enemy ...

(a) Once he had invented light
(b) The 'Lord of the land' is now more commonly known as a 'landlord'
(c) 'You' is equal to every man, woman and child who has ever been born
(d) *See* the Bible for terms and conditions

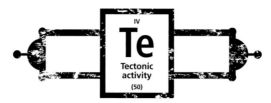

IV

Te

Tectonic
activity

(50)

Tectonic activity. *tek·ton·ik··ak·tivity* – the Earth's crust is made up of different layers that push together or pull apart. Known as plate tectonics, this action gives humankind a bumpy ride.

The world is like an impossible jigsaw puzzle that can never be completed as the pieces eventually change in shape and size. In the olden days, the land mass of the Earth was one single super-sized jigsaw piece but, over billions of years, the Earth's tectonic plates have moved to their current position, causing the countries up above to migrate. Even though they don't look like it, the continents are just passing through on their continual journey.

The effects of this movement are both good and bad: good when the plates push together,[1] which causes the land to rise forming beautiful mountains, but bad when the Earth is ripped apart, causing rifts that vent lava and trigger earthquakes, as your town falls into the hole. It's not all bad news, as these rifts can be many miles long, forming new land to build your new town on. But even though the tectonic activity is a slow process, if the plates rupture in various key danger spots around the globe, it could trigger a flood basalt eruption[2] with consequences felt the world over.

WHEN WILL IT HAPPEN?

The tectonic plates are moving right now.

With every tremor, earthquake or volcanic eruption the plates are tearing apart or coming together.

Continents are slowly getting bigger or smaller. One country's extension is another's demolition.

WHEN SHOULD I START TO PANIC?

Later, you've already got enough on your plate as it is.

WHAT SHOULD I LOOK FOR?

The red innards of the Earth spewing out. New land where there was once sea. Sea where there was once old land. New mountains or lakes, very shaky ground, lava where towns and cities used to be. Massive lava pits where entire countries used to be.

---

1. As long as it doesn't kill you • 2. *See* Volcanic activity (54)

tektonikus great britannicus
Mainly seen in Europe but was once spotted on the other side of the Atlantic Ocean.

tektonikus australicus
Once seen near the South Pole, it can now be seen on the edge of the Indian, Southern and Pacific oceans.

tektonikus chinacus
Has a massive presence in Asia.

tektonikus indianica
Travelled rapidly from the globe's most southern point until it came to be a permanent fixture in Asia.

tektonikus amerikus
Once an equatorial resident of the now extinct Iapetus Ocean, this land mass united with a ex-resident of Gondwana to form the Americas.

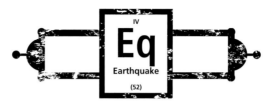

IV

Eq
Earthquake
(52)

Earthquake. *erff·qwake* – **when you feel the Earth move and it has nothing to do with sex.**

Have you ever had a truly embarrassing moment and wished that the world would open up and swallow you whole? Well, be very, very careful what you wish for. Our world is constantly on the move. There's estimated to be one earthquake every thirty seconds somewhere in the world, so when the Earth starts to bust a move you know it'll be dancing to the sound of rock 'n' roll. To avoid being woken up at all hours by the Earth's partying, you'd best move as far away as possible from any fractures in the Earth's crust.[1] You're safer inland. You may find that you can still feel them there, but the magnitude of the quake will be much reduced. By staying close to a coastal fault line you risk the threat of severe tremors, devastating earthquakes, landslides and tsunamis, especially if there is a seaquake.[2]

WHEN WILL IT HAPPEN?

It can happen anytime, anyplace, anywhere.
  The Earth is constantly suffering from growing pains.

WILL I FEEL THE EARTH MOVE?

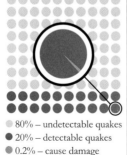

○ 80% – undetectable quakes
● 20% – detectable quakes
● 0.2% – cause damage

Source: U.S. Geological Survey

WHEN SHOULD I START TO PANIC?

LATER · TOO LATE · NOW · SOON

Depends where you live. If you live in a place with a history of earthquakes, like San Francisco, you should have panicked and moved away already. The warning signs are in this city's history. If you don't heed them, it won't all be San Andreas' fault.

WHAT SHOULD I LOOK FOR?

The familiar surroundings that you know and love moving in an unfamiliar and destructive way. Massive holes appearing around you. A pile of firewood and debris where your house used to be. Explosions, and fire. Apocalyptic scenes and possibly a wall of water.

WHAT SHOULD I DO NEXT?

There's nowhere you can run to. Even the Moon suffers from moonquakes.

---

1. *See* Tectonic activity (50) • 2. *See* Tsunami (60)

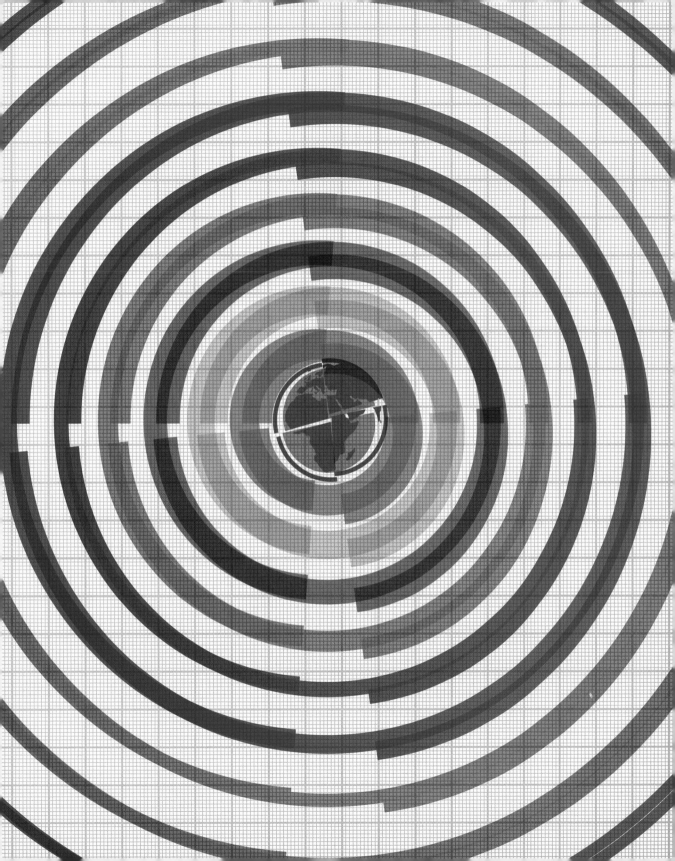

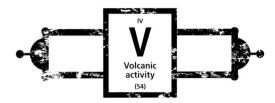

IV
V
Volcanic activity
(54)

Volcanic activity. *vol·kan·nik··ak·tivity* – volcanism relates to the internal processes of a volcano, usually resulting in an eruption. These processes are not to be confused with Vulcanism: a belief in the philosophies of dedicated Spock fans, usually involving dressing up and wearing pointy ears.

The prevalence of volcanoes on Earth is predominately related to the boundaries of the tectonic plates;[1] the closer you are to a boundary, the more likely you are to have a volcano pop up in your neighbourhood.[2]

You don't hear of volcanoes erupting every day – if no one dies, the world doesn't want to know. But hear of a big eruption with communities under threat and, while the locals are fleeing the lava, you can guarantee an influx of news helicopters circling the ash plume like a swarm of bees protecting their honey-rich home from an invading bear.

And you don't have to have a volcano in your back garden for it to kill you stone dead, it depends on what kind of volcano it is. It could be on the other side of the world and still take you out. When you think of a volcano, you'll probably imagine the familiar conical protrusion sticking out of the ground with its early-warning system of smoke signals,[3] but these boys are volcanic decoys, they're taking the heat for supervolcanoes, the big brothers of volcanism.

Supervolcanoes had been in hiding for centuries until scientists in the 1960s uncovered their refuge. It turns out that they had been right under our noses all along, disguised as floor. The first supervolcano was discovered hiding under the lake of Yellowstone National Park.

The supervolcano is massive, making the more familiar volcanoes look like molehills in comparison. The Yellowstone caldera[4] is estimated to be 55 km by 72 km wide. So, how come it took so long to find it? Was the Old Faithful Geyser not a big enough clue that

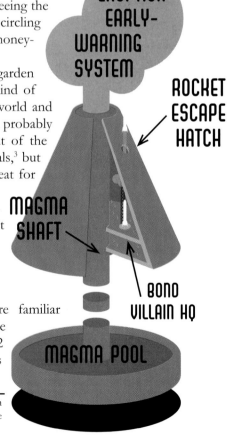

ERUPTION EARLY-WARNING SYSTEM

ROCKET ESCAPE HATCH

MAGMA SHAFT

BOND VILLAIN HQ

MAGMA POOL

1. *See* Tectonic activity (50) • 2. *See* the movie *Volcano* (1997) ... actually, on second thoughts ... don't • 3. Ignore the signals at your peril, just ask the

something was up, or rather under? If this bad boy erupts, God help us. Millions, if not all of us, will die.

The gas and magma that lie under the Earth's surface are compressed, so much so that the ground above will rise upwards due to the huge pressure the contents below are under. If the pressure becomes too great, the escape hatch will be blown and the compacted gas and magma will expand, bursting through the ground into the atmosphere, whilst turning thousands of square miles into a sea of lava.

If you're in the Yellowstone area and you're thinking of eloping to the other side of the world, be aware that the cloud of ash, gas and debris that'll be ejected into the atmosphere will hunt you down. It will block out the sun, causing a global darkness in the corner of the world you've chosen to hide in and turning the rain toxic. Not only that, the temperature of the Earth will plummet, killing crops, livestock and, ultimately, us. So you may as well stay put and wait for the big red tidal wave. After all, Yellowstone isn't the only supervolcano playing hide-and-seek, there are more around the world being uncovered. So until they reveal themselves by erupting and taking your entire country away, you might as well sit tight and wait for the fireworks.

WHEN WILL IT HAPPEN?

There are around fifty to sixty volcanic eruptions every month, although a supervolcano hasn't erupted for tens of thousands of years. On the downside, it has been estimated that a Yellowstone explosion is long overdue.

WHAT SHOULD I LOOK FOR?

The ground under your feet swelling, a strange smell in the air, the lake you're in getting hotter and turning from blue to red.

WHEN SHOULD I START TO PANIC?

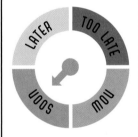

Start quietly moving out of any regions that boast calderas and start stocking your panic room with essentials. Ultimately, when the day turns to night and stays this way for years on end, it's far too late for panicking.

A LESSON FROM HISTORY

An area called the Deccan Traps had been erupting in India around the same time as the asteroid struck, signalling the end of the dinosaurs approximately 65 million years ago.

Approximately one million cubic kilometres were covered in lava, triggering the release of greenhouse gases. With the combination of the erupting traps and the asteroid, the dinosaurs were wiped out.

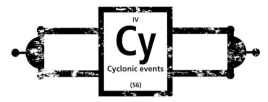

IV

Cy

Cyclonic events

(56)

Cyclonic events. *si·klon·ik··e·vents* – a circular wind system, aka cyclone, anticyclone, hurricane, typhoon, tropical storm, whirlwind, tornado, twister, willy willy or even Gary. Whatever you want to call it, it's going to be one hell of a bad hair day.

Whatever the name,[1] all of the above are classed as cyclonic events. As the effects of global warming bite, we're informed that these destructive blustery beasts are going to get much more powerful and the parts that usually escape their wrath are beginning to suffer. The number of category-five storms is due to increase, as is their ferocity. The planet has seen the most category-five storms in a decade and it's been suggested that a sixth category be added to the Hurricane Scale as they become increasingly bad-ass. With plenty more violent storms predicted, we're in for a wet and wild time, there's definitely something brewing ... keep an eye on the storm.

WHEN WILL IT HAPPEN?

We're already getting a taste of what's to become 'normal' as our contributions to global warming have inadvertently upgraded these events to super-cyclonic.

WHAT SHOULD I LOOK FOR?

Clouds that can rival any apocalyptic Bible illustration. Howling winds, horizontal rain, flooding, thunderbolts lightning, tidal waves, uprooted trees, flying people and cows.

WHEN SHOULD I START TO PANIC?

Batten down the hatches and brace yourself for an ass-whipping from the winds. If it ain't tethered down, prepare to lose it. Even if it is tethered down there is still no guarantee it'll survive the storms that are brewing ...

WHAT WEATHER CAN WE EXPECT?

WHAT'S THE STORM DAMAGE?

Expect the following damage (per category):
1: Not significant.
2: Some damage.
3: Structural damage.
4: Heavy damage.
5: Significant damage.
6: Utter carnage.

---

1. A storm system's name depends on various factors, including the atmospheric pressure, temperature, width. Or it could be down to what part of the world it decides to attack

El Niño and La Niña. *el·neen·yo·· and·· la·neen·ya* – **the evil twins of the world's weather system.**

El Niño and La Niña (Spanish for 'little boy' and 'little girl') are the split personalities of the Southern Oscillation – a naturally occurring phenomenon caused by temperature fluctuations within the sea that manifests itself as two types of storm systems – a harsh and arid La Niña is born out of cold conditions and a stormy El Niño is born out of warm. Just like a person with a split personality, El Niño and La Niña never make an appearance at the same time, one exists while the other stays dormant, and they have very different effects.

El Niño manifests itself every two to five years, and is the cause of floods and droughts. This event can cause cows to die of thirst on one side of the ocean and it can flood everyone else on the other side. In between the little boy's outbursts, we feel the little girl's anger. La Niña has the opposite effect, making wet places wetter and dry places drier. The effects are usually manageable, but every now and again one of the twins becomes totally uncontrollable, leaving a trail of destruction in its wake. Combine this with global warming and strengthening storms and we can soon expect many more twin tantrums.[1]

WHEN WILL IT HAPPEN?	WHEN SHOULD I START TO PANIC?	POSSIBILITY IT WILL HAPPEN?
El Niño has been occurring every two to five years for thousands of years. La Niña makes an appearance on the little boy's days off.		100%. These Oscillations have been happening for centuries and it doesn't look like they're going to stop terrorising us anytime soon.
WHAT SHOULD I LOOK FOR?		**AKA**
Rain when it should be clear and clear sky when it should be raining.	You know when to expect it and what is going to occur so be prepared.	El Niño: The Little Boy or Christ child. La Niña: The Little Girl or El Viejo.

1. *See* Warming seas (106)

What are little boys made of?
Floods and storms and heavy rainfalls
That's what little boys are made of...

What are little girls made of?
Cold and drought, without a doubt
That's what little girls are made of...

IV

Ts

Tsunami

(60)

Tsunami. *sue·nah·me* – when the sea turns from horizontal to vertical.

The oceans of the world are pretty nervous characters. On the face of it they present a cool, dead-calm exterior, but given a short sharp shock they run a mile.[1] Any sudden surprises like an earthquake, landslide, glacier collapse, volcanic eruption or an asteroid impact and they run for the hills, literally.

A tsunami, or 'harbour wave' in Japanese, starts as an area of displaced water that travels, in some cases hundreds of miles, before it reaches the coast. When it arrives at the shallows, the upper part of the wave is travelling faster than the lower. It starts to gain in size, drawing in the water away from the beach. The *agitated water*[2] of a tsunami ends with an enormous all-engulfing wave that crashes on to the shore and travels inland for many miles, consuming anything and anyone that gets in its way.

But that isn't the half of it: an even bigger wave, known as a mega tsunami, can be generated by landslides. These types of wave are rare but they do happen and the fighting talk from scientists predicts that a mega tsunami could, one day, be generated by a landslide that could take down New York. Oh yeah, you and whose tsunami?

WHEN WILL IT HAPPEN?

Impossible to predict as a seaquake can strike at any time. Early-warning systems are put in place to give people a chance to escape a surprise tsunami attack.

WHAT SHOULD I LOOK FOR?

Sea where the sky used to be.

WHEN SHOULD I START TO PANIC?

Too late if you're at the seaside. Later if you live on a hill.

YOU AND WHOSE TSUNAMI?

The volcanic island of La Palma is unstable. If it erupts again, it could trigger a landslide that, in the worst case, will generate a mega tsunami that will travel across the Pacific Ocean and strike the shores of Northern and Southern America, Africa and Europe.

---

1. Never invite an ocean to watch a horror movie with you otherwise you'll be drowned in your own home • 2. *See* Water (20)

Wildfire. *why·eld·fyar* – the uncontrollable power of man's red flower.

Fire has been the adopted child of humankind since some bright spark first tamed it and made it dance for our entertainment on the tips of candles. It entertained, heated and guided us through the centuries but of late, fire has fallen out of favour due to a usurper, the lightbulb.

Fire is still a key part in our lives but for all its good points it has a major downside: when it becomes wild, it's completely uncontrollable. Fire has turned on us time after time and has destroyed our towns and cities on numerous occasions. Famously, a bored and ignored dying flame took revenge on a sleeping baker in 1666 and raged for three days, taking most of London with it. Modern-day wildfires easily take hold in the dry forests of summertime – the perfect environment for fires to run wild. In recent times the Blue Mountains of Australia have turned orange, Portugal and Spain have seen red and Hollywood has burned just like the disaster movies it churns out.

In our ever-warming world, rainfall is becoming unevenly distributed,[1] forests are becoming drier, creating more fires. More fires equal more CO_2 making fires more frequent. Wildfires are going to kick up a firestorm: with a huff and a puff, they'll burn your house down.

WHEN WILL IT HAPPEN?

When it's not just the streetlights in your neighbourhood that have an orange glow.

WHAT SHOULD I LOOK FOR?

Dancing orange[2] light-emitting protuberances that vary in size from tens of millimetres to tens of metres.

WHEN SHOULD I START TO PANIC?

Fire is easy to start but hard to stop. You may have met your match.

WHAT SHOULD I DO NEXT?

Stay well back. The closer you get the hotter you will become. Do not feed the flames as the fire will continue to burn longer. Do not fan the flames as the fire will spread. If you ignore the fire it may go away of its own accord but this is optimistic and doubtful.

---

1. Via intense storms rather than gradually over long periods • 2. Please note: flame colour may vary

V

Turned out ice again

Turned out ice again *ternd·owt·eys·ag·ayne* **– when it's cold enough to snow and snow and snow ...**

The Earth is like a faulty old refrigerator with a temperamental thermostat: sometimes it gets far too hot or far too cold. With its door closed and the thermostat behaving itself, the fridge will freeze in the right places. If the thermostat misbehaves and turns colder, the entire compartment will cool further, causing ice to form where it shouldn't. This ice will grow and creep towards the door, engulfing the vegetables and condiments in its path, causing a mini ice age containing carrots and peas instead of buildings and people. Forget to defrost the fridge and it'll completely freeze, just like a snowball Earth scenario.[1]

On the other hand, if the thermostat switches to high the ice will retreat and no new ice will form, causing your vegetables to go off and die, just like the predicted effects of global warming. Either way, you're going to have one hell of a job either defrosting or mopping up your Earth's kitchen.

---

1. 650 million years ago it's believed that the Earth completely froze like a giant snowball. At the time, the planet wasn't warm enough to hold back the ice due to a lack of carbon dioxide in the atmosphere to heat the planet and the ice sheet grew right across the planet on an unstoppable ice rampage

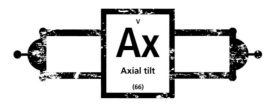

Ax
v
Axial tilt
(66)

Axial tilt. *ax·eel··tilt* – when the Earth doesn't sit up straight.

As we pass through space on our year-long procession around the Sun, the Earth spins on its axis over a twenty-four-hour period. The Earth is vertically challenged and is currently leaning at a laid-back angle of 23.5°, but it isn't static and fluctuates between 22.1° and 24.5° over a 41,000-year period. These angles are the reason for the seasons. Although a degree change of around 2.5° doesn't sound much, this little fluctuation has a big consequence. At the moment the angle of the Earth is decreasing, so we're heading away from the hotter summers and colder winters of 24.5° and heading towards the cooler summers and colder winters of 22° but due to rapid climate change the Earth is heading towards the 24.5° temperatures at breakneck speed within decades, even though it should get colder over the next 20,000 years. By the time the Earth reaches the 22° mark, the northern hemisphere will look like it's wearing a badly fitted white toupée that falls over the eyes of London, New York and Moscow for thousands of years. Add in other factors like the Earth's eccentricity,[1] its wobble[2] and a hint of global warming and we've got a recipe for disaster the next major ice age may be cancelled. We'd prefer our planet's temperature to stay the way Goldilocks prefers her porridge, but it looks like we have to get used to our planet being far too hot. At least Goldilocks had a choice: even the too cold option seems quite appealing.

WHEN WILL IT HAPPEN?

In thousands of years, soon[3] or never again. It's down to the many moods of global warming.

WHAT SHOULD I LOOK FOR?

If snow was rare in your part of the world and now the view is usually white, welcome to a new ice age.

WHEN SHOULD I START TO PANIC?

Sooner or later. When an ice age starts, run away at full tilt.

WHAT SHOULD I DO NEXT?

Look for the Moon. The Moon keeps the Earth's rotation stable via gravitational effects.

If the moon suddenly vanished[4] then the Earth would spin uncontrollably.

Within a very short period of time America could become the new 'Down Under'.

---

1. The eccentricity of the Earth is the variation in its orbital cycle that alters over a 100,000-year period
2. The wobble causes the seasons' effects to peak every 23,000 years • 3. *See* Gulf stream collapse (116)
4. *See* Moon (228)

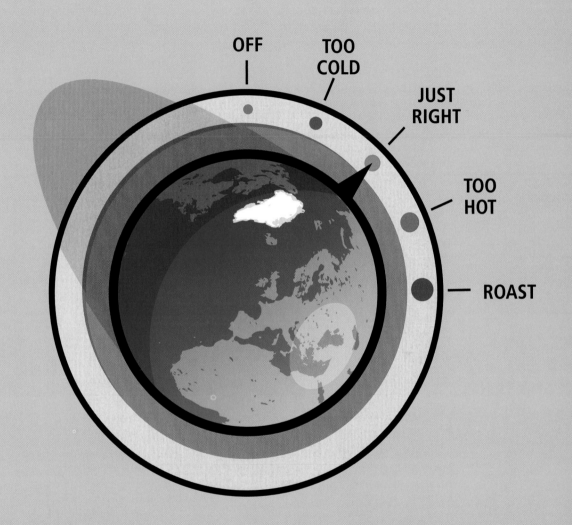

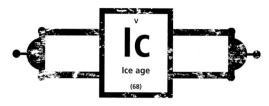

Ic

v

Ice age

(68)

Ice age. *eyes··ayj* – when a wall of ice journeys south from the North Pole into northern Europe, Asia and North America. After stretching for a few thousand years, it heads back north.

With talk of the planet warming up it's surprising to find out that the planet is actually going through an ice epoch.[1] This current period, that started over 1.8 million years ago and carries on up to present day, is called the quaternary glaciation, which refers to the permanent ice sheets residing at both poles.

When an ice age does kick in, it will lock up most of the world's fresh water supplies, causing the sea levels to drop and droughts to occur in the hotter parts of the world. Mountain ranges around the planet will also trap snow and millions of people in the northern hemisphere would be displaced due to the advancing ice from the North Pole. In the next ice age, the ice will slowly begin to encroach southwards during icy cold winter months and it'll retreat less during the cooler summers.

Year in, year out, the ice will slowly creep south. The advancing ice will head beyond the Arctic circle, down past London, visiting all the towns and countries in between, crushing their famous attractions underneath its feet, hundreds of feet of frozen ice.

WHEN WILL IT HAPPEN?

Hopefully not yet. Put your survival gear order back on the wish list.

WHAT SHOULD I LOOK FOR?

Very white Christmases and July 4ths. Polar bears in London, Caribou in New York and ice where Canada used to be.

WHEN SHOULD I START TO PANIC?

It depends on what will trigger the next ice age first ...

WHAT HAPPENS NEXT?

The next ice age caused by the Earth's axial tilt[2] isn't due for about another 15,000 years but there is a theory that it could be triggered sooner by the collapse of the North Atlantic gulf stream.[3]

If this theory is correct then start panicking very soon indeed.

---

1. An ice epoch is a colder period of time that can contain warmer interglacial periods between ice ages. We are currently in a interglacial period • 2. *See* Axial tilt (66) • 3. *See* Gulf stream collapse (116)

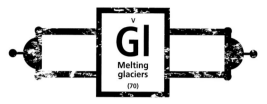

GI
∨
Melting glaciers
(70)

Melting glaciers. *mel·ting··glass·syers* – when the world's refrigerators begin leaking, causing the kitchen to flood.

Just like the Wicked Witch of the West, the glaciers of the world are melting. Ten per cent of the Earth's land is currently occupied by glaciers but just like an ice lolly that has been dropped on the floor, they're letting go of their flavour and water content. Whiteland, to the east of Canada, is almost entirely covered in glaciers. If the glaciers melt then Whiteland will have to be renamed Greenland at great expense to map makers worldwide.[1] The melted water from the glaciers collects in pools on top of the ice, it burrows down to the bedrock through cracks, weakening the glacier further, causing sections to give way and become seaborne. This process is accelerating each year and soon all we'll have left to show for our ice caps will be two enormous floating wooden sticks, but the joke will be on us.

WHEN WILL IT HAPPEN?

It's happening now. There's more crushed ice in the sea than in a sea breeze cocktail.

WHAT SHOULD I LOOK FOR?

A vast ice cube heading in your direction.

As a glacier breaks apart, you'll hear enormous and eerie cracking noises just before it lets go. If the ice has already gone, then you'll find a huge gorge where the ice used to be with a big puddle at the bottom.

WHEN SHOULD I START TO PANIC?

The majority of the world's glaciers are melting, some faster than others. If the fresh waters of the Greenland glaciers reach the sea it could accelerate the collapse of the gulf stream.[2] Not good. Let's try to keep the glaciers on ice.

WATER, WATER EVERYWHERE

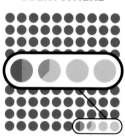

● 97.5% of the world's water is salty sea

●● The other 2.5% of the world's water is fresh which compromises of ice, snow, rain, lakes, rivers or underground (75% of all fresh water)

● 2.625% of the world's water is locked up in glaciers

Source: NSIDC/WWF

---

1. You may own a world map with this change already made • 2. *See* Gulf stream collapse (116)

Se

v

Sea ice

(72)

Sea ice. *see··iz* – the receding hairline of the Earth's frozen water scalp and nether regions.

The ice of the Arctic is continually advancing and retreating depending on the season, but during the summer months of the last few years, vast expanses of sea have appeared where the sea ice used to be. Sea ice reflects around 85% of the sun's rays whereas open sea reflects only around 10% of the rays and absorbs the rest, so the more open sea there is, the more heat is absorbed, accelerating the melting further. We'll soon have a bubbling hot bath at the roof of our Earth for the fish instead of a frozen ice-box. The newly melted ice will join forces with the already fluid sea on their mission to rise up and create a new wet room with some of the coastal and low-lying land.[1] So be prepared for the new seaside to now be beside your bedside table as the rising seas will have to go somewhere.

WHEN WILL IT HAPPEN?

While one of the poles freezes in winter, the other is melting in the summer. The summer sea in the Arctic is like a tall cocktail full of crushed ice, except the ingredients are unusual, making it taste a little fishy.

WHAT SHOULD I LOOK FOR?

A lot more blue where there was once a lot of white. Polar bears, penguins and arctic foxes looking more conspicuous than usual.

WHEN SHOULD I START TO PANIC?

It was once predicted that the Arctic Ocean would be ice free by 2080. Then the year was decreased to 2050, then 2030. The latest prediction is that the summer sea ice will disappear within twenty years. We'll soon be able to see if they're right.

WHAT SHOULD I DO NEXT?

If sea levels start to rise then we should look to Archimedes and his findings on water displacement for a solution. If an object is placed in water it will displace it by causing the level to rise. The same applies to the fresh water from the melting ice. If you notice a rise in sea level, go fishing and remove as many fish and mammals out of the sea as possible to gain an equilibrium.[2] Be warned, Eu'll reka after handling all that fish.

---

1. *See* Rising sea levels (118) • 2. *See* Food chain collapse (92)

VI

Silent but deadly

Silent but deadly. *sy·lent··butt··ded·leigh* – when the Earth stealthily purges the land of human life.

The Earth is out to get us whichever way it can. It employs big and brash 'Acts of God'[1] to intimidate and eliminate us, but when the big guns don't work as anticipated, our crafty planet can resort to sneakier tactics to try to wipe us out. With a little patience, the Earth can bide its time and eliminate some of us with more stealth.

Across the face of the planet there are areas that can naturally cause humans some serious grief, and in the worst case death. On their own they may seem of little importance but combined with the gathering global warming storm, the Earth is quietly drawing up its plans against us that can be silent but very, very deadly.

---

1. *See* Acts of God (48)

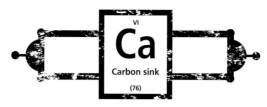

VI
Ca
Carbon sink
(76)

Carbon sink. *karbon·sync* – when the rainforests and the oceans store carbon dioxide extracted from the air, which is eventually turned into a carbon belch, poisoning us with noxious fumes.

Breathing in someone else's stale air isn't nice but it's fine if you're a tree. Like non-smokers breathing in secondary smoke, trees are inhaling our noxious fumes. They absorb the polluting filth that we pump out without question and, as luck would have it, the trees and the plants seem to like it. While we're expelling unwanted CO_2, the plants and trees soak it up and turn it into oxygen through photosynthesis for us to breathe. This is all very handy: the trees inhale what we exhale and vice versa, a perfect partnership that's been going on for millions for years. For us, the more you consume without exercising, the more weight you put on and this is also true for the trees. It's been discovered that the trees of the world's rainforests are starting to get a little tubby through the consumption of CO_2. Trees can't exercise, so they have a very different way of losing weight, which, unfortunately for us, causes the planet's air fresheners to turn toxic. The trees and seas that've been absorbing the CO_2 will have a limit,[1] and drinking to excess will inevitably lead to throwing up, resulting in the trees' excess gas being released into the atmosphere and the oceans turning acidic. The carbon sink is soon to become our very own the carbon stink.

WHEN WILL IT HAPPEN?

We're producing all the ingredients for the excess CO_2 to be released back into the wild very soon.

WHAT SHOULD I LOOK FOR?

Trees losing weight. Clouds of gas rising above the canopy that isn't water vapour.

WHEN SHOULD I START TO PANIC?

It may be better out than in for the trees ... but not for us.

SOMETHING IN THE AIR (%)

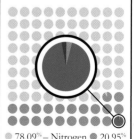

78.09% – Nitrogen 20.95% – Oxygen 0.93% – Argon 0.03% – CO_2 0.003% – Trace elements inc. water vapour

Source: Weather questions.com

---

1. Other factors that can cause the release of CO_2 back into the atmosphere are forest fires, the soil drying out, and decay; deforesting doesn't help either. At least new trees suck up CO_2 faster than the old boys do, so get planting as fast as you can.

Me
VI
Methane
sink
(78)

Methane sink. *meeth·ayne··sync* – when the sea and the Earth collectively fart, giving us a massive headache.

If you thought breathing in the bad breath of the trees was bad enough,[1] wait until you get a lung full of the excess gas of the seas and the Earth. While the trees are soaking up our air pollution, the Earth and the seas are soaking up methane gas as well as CO_2. Methane is produced by bacteria that thrive on organic matter. As the matter from flora or fauna breaks down, methane is released into the atmosphere or emitted straight into your nostrils via a fellow passenger's rotten intestines on a packed tube train. Methane sinks are areas across the world where tons of the gas becomes trapped in the earth via soil or bogs, in water via ice or lake- and seabeds; the rest of the methane that escapes burial collects in the troposphere. Methane is around 23% more harmful than carbon dioxide, so we don't want the trapped methane to be released back into the wild, but that's exactly what is expected to happen. As the temperature increases, the gas escapes from the melting ice via air bubbles in the peat bogs trapped underneath the enormous Siberian tundra as it defrosts. The trapped gas in the seabed could heat up and be released from its watery prison into the air, heating the Earth even further. These are the type of blocked sink we'll be happy to see bunged up.

WHEN WILL IT HAPPEN?

It's already happening. Methane is escaping from the sinks as the planet thaws out. If the planet's temperature keeps rising, more methane will be released, which will raise the temperature further, escalating the changes and taking us to a very hot land of no return.

WHEN SHOULD I START TO PANIC?

Now, but it could already be too late. Time to put a bung in it.[2]

WHAT SHOULD I LOOK FOR?

Methane is a highly flammable gas so if you see the strange phenomenon of fire coming from ice you'll know the sink has become unblocked.

Also keep an eye out for oceans and lakes bubbling like a jacuzzi, or dead animals littering the ground.

1. *See* Carbon sink (76) • 2. *See* Animal flatulence (94)

VI

De

Desertification

(80)

Desertification. *dez·er·tif·ik·a·shon* – when a man's home becomes his sandcastle.

For those who can't wait to hit the beach, if you hang around long enough the beach might come and hit you. Desertification is the result of many varied factors, including over farming, deforestation and our old enemy, climate change. It can turn once fertile land into a giant sandpit. The sand-dunes that form through desertification bully their next-door neighbours, giving a new meaning to having sand kicked in your face. The dunes grow in size and once the wind has whipped the sand up into a storm, it heads off on a rampage. Millions of tons of sand mix with the winds and tear across thousands of miles, depositing yellow grit along the way. Over time, the sand builds up and slowly encroaches on towns and villages, eventually pushing out the residents. The ghost towns that remain will slowly be buried under the sand, so if life isn't already a beach for you, it soon could be. The process has been happening around the world for centuries but with the world hotting up, it may accelerate. Ancient cities are being discovered and modern wonders of the world like the Great Wall of China are being threatened with burial. It seems that wherever it lays its sandbags, that's its home.

WHEN WILL IT HAPPEN?

Now. Green and fertile lands are turning yellow.

WHAT SHOULD I LOOK FOR?

Enormous dirty clouds that smother you in yellow snow. A stinging sensation in your eyes and an ability to build sandcastles in your once thriving garden pond.

WHEN SHOULD I START TO PANIC?

The sands of time are falling. If it's not too late, it's a matter of time.

DESERTIFICATION CERTIFICATION

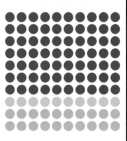

● 70% of the Earth is water
●● 30% of the Earth is land
● 10% of the Earth is desert

Source: Oxfam

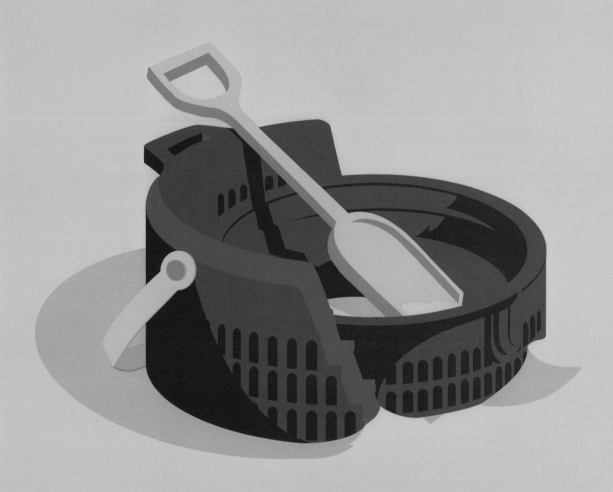

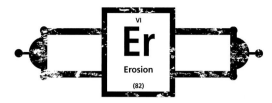

VI
Er
Erosion
(82)

Erosion. *ee·row·shon* – when the sea gnaws, the Earth moves and the Heavens open.

What little amount of land we have to live on is being looked upon with envious eyes. Our land is being attacked from all sides by a very jealous sea. This massive and eternally hungry body of water is slowly taking bite-sized chunks of our coastlines, hoping that we won't notice, in a bid to reclaim the land that once appeared out of its depths. The sea's relentless waves are like continually renewing sets of teeth gnawing at the land, and with over 221,000 miles of coastline in the world, that's a lot of nibbling. But the sea is capable of more than just amphibious assaults: it can also penetrate the land through a series of air raids, as water from the oceans is air-lifted up into the atmosphere where it creates a formation of clouds that are ready to deploy their water cargo down on the rocks and the soil of this land at will. The land invasion can come in varying degrees, from light rain raids through to heavy blanket bombings, randomly deployed throughout the year. The resulting saturation causes the land to weather and erode, which in turn can cause devastating mud- and landslides. And not even the massive hills and mountains are safe from the water blitz that pounds their craggy faces. With a little help from its friends[1] and given enough time, the weather-beaten mountains will eventually be worn down to tiny naked nubbies, making a molehill out of a mountain.

WHEN WILL IT HAPPEN?	WHEN SHOULD I START TO PANIC?	POSSIBILITY IT WILL HAPPEN?
The hungry sea is constantly chomping its way up the world's coastline, devouring the land as it goes but luckily for us it can be a very VERY slow process. Look out for an envious ocean racked with jealous sea.	 Don't redraw the map yet.	If you live within a few miles of the coast make sure your sea defences are in order: you'll need to fight erosion on the beaches. Even if you live inland your property may one day end up beside the seaside, or, worse still, actually in the sea.

1. The Sun, heat, frost, pressure, salt, chemicals, certain organisms and the wind

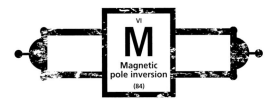

VI

M
Magnetic pole inversion
(84)

Magnetic pole inversion. *mag·net·tick··poll··in·ver·chon* – when your compass points south instead of north.

The interior of the Earth is a massive swirling ball of molten iron that creates a magnetic field around the planet as it churns, giving our planet a north and south pole, just like a magnet. Even though it's called a north pole in name, in nature the magnetic version doesn't reside in the same place as the main north pole at the top of the world as it isn't static. It roams across parts of the northern hemisphere at over 40 km in a year and is currently swimming with the fishes under the Arctic sea ice on a course for Siberia. That's the problem with the magnetic pole: it can sometimes stray very far from home, sometimes far too far. The Earth is like a giant magnet without the attractiveness. When you drop something metal it's attracted to the floor by gravity[1] and not magnetism, as the Earth's magnetic field is weak and getting weaker all the time. If it becomes too weak it's entirely possible for the poles to swap places, north becomes south and vice versa. Although there won't be any lasting effects to our lives it'll confuse your compass and any animals that happen to be migrating at the time. If you wake up and find buffalo in your garden then you'll know that the magnetic pole has completely flipped out.

WHEN WILL IT HAPPEN?

Soon. The poles are long overdue a flipping.

WHAT SHOULD I LOOK FOR?

Confused birds flying south for the summer and north for the winter, wildebeest with no sense of direction and vultures circling anti-clockwise.

WHEN SHOULD I START TO PANIC?

Later ... there shouldn't be any lasting negative, or positive, effects.

WHAT SHOULD I DO NEXT?

As it shouldn't affect us, keep an eye on compasses. They'll be showing very unusual readings.
  Tag birds and migratory animals and track their progress across the world. Their journeys may resemble the random trails a snail leaves behind it.

1. *See* Gravity (220)

VII
Wild life

Wild life *why·ald··lye·fff* – the living organisms that crawl across the Earth's surface.

Since the arrival of the very first single-cell organisms, Earth's creatures have endured attempts on their lives from many different sources. They've almost been wiped out by asteroids, been cooked by supervolcanoes, endured hot periods of global warming and survived the cold of a planet that froze entirely, but each time, life, in its various incarnations, bounces back. It has evolved into the many spectacular and unique beasts that have been lucky enough to live to tell the tale. What we're left with today are the descendants of those perennial survivors that didn't bite the dust or meet their maker. One species – ours – has risen up above the rest and single-handedly tamed, defeated or wrestled the rest of the creatures for their meat, fur, fins, oil, bones, beauty or habitat. But the animals of Earth's pet shop, discovered and undiscovered, may have the last laugh: their extinction will ultimately lead to ours.

BORDERS.

BORDERS
BOOKS MUSIC AND CAFE
3539 E. Main
St. Charles, IL 60174
(630) 443-8160

STORE: 0408   REG: 03/97 TRAN#: 6546
SALE   12/23/2010 EMP: 00030

GIFT RECEIPT

A IS FOR ARMAGEDDON
     3178369   QP T   CFFM

ILLINOIS 8.0%   TAX

12/23/2010 02:24PM

VII
Eco
Ecosystem
(88)

Ecosystem. *ee·ko·sis·tem* – when the animals, plants and their habitats got along harmoniously, until humankind magically appeared ... and put the harm in harmonious.

The world's ecosystem is a community of living organisms that interact with each other and the surrounding environment. Animals, plants, birds, insects and every other living organism rely on each other, for better or worse, which keeps the whole wheel of life turning. But humankind has turned the wheel of life into a fast-spinning wheel of death. The lucky species avoid the daggers of extinction being thrown at them, although they're getting closer each time, whereas the unlucky ones take direct hits and, to add insult to injury, we're even killing species we haven't even met yet. According to WWF, less than two million species have been found, named and catalogued but there could be anywhere between 10 and 50 million undiscovered species still out there[1] in the undergrowth and treetops. The extinction rate is now up to 1,000 times higher than the normal rate of extinction,[2] which equals an estimated 10,000 extinctions a year. That's some disappearing act but, unfortunately, there are no impressive puffs of smoke or reappearances like rabbits from magicians' hats. Species are disappearing from Earth quicker than you can say abra-cadaver. Now that's *not* magic!

WHEN WILL IT HAPPEN?

The delicate balance of the ecosystem is being upset by the food chain collapse, pollution and deforestation, amongst many other factors.

WHAT SHOULD I LOOK FOR?

Anything with a face. Green trees, grasses, plants turning brown.

WHEN SHOULD I START TO PANIC?

Start your very own Eden Project. Turn your house into a nature reserve.

WHAT WILL HAPPEN NEXT?

The last of the planet's creatures are slithering, scurrying and flying up the stairway to animal Heaven at an alarming rate.[3]

99% of all species that have ever lived are already on the upstairs landing, let's not force the final 1% up the dancers.[4]

---

1. Although 10 million undiscovered species is a best guesstimate • 2. *See* Extinction (6) • 3. Based on fossil records, the normal rate of extinction is one species in a million per year • 4. The stairways to animal Heaven were originally designed to accommodate animals two by two; they've now been modified to accommodate many more as they've got a stampede on their hands

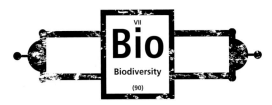

VII
Bio
Biodiversity
(90)

Biodiversity. *buy·o·die·verse·sit·tee* – the sum of all living organisms within an ecosystem. But the sums are beginning to feature more minus signs than they used too.

It's OK to be different, and in the case of biodiversity, it's essential. The biodiversity of an area props up the entire ecosystem: remove one element from the equation and the organisms that relied on that one missing species will go hungry, move on or die.[1] But the opposite is also true: if the species that has been removed was a top predator, then another species will claim the crown, which could be even more devastating. It's a similar story if a new species is introduced to the region – it could quite easily wreak havoc on the environment. A harmless bug introduced from South America could thrive and destroy the biodiversity of Europe, or vice versa. The plants and creatures that used to be at the top of the food chain can be overthrown and slip down, or even off, the list. These non-indigenous species can find their way into new countries and run wild via intentional[2] or accidental introduction, or in the case of plants, the seed may have been brought in by wind or water. So when your garden begins to look like a scene from *Jumanji* and carnivorous Triffids[3] are breaking down your door to make you their breakfast, you'll regret the day you bought those

WHAT SHOULD I LOOK FOR?

Your favourite plants disappearing from the landscape.

Unfamiliar plants or creatures that you've never seen before.

Be wary of large poisonous plants with heads reminiscent of angry orchids. Be warned, these plants can walk. Shoot to kill.

WHEN SHOULD I START TO PANIC?

Fee! Fie! Foe! Fum! I smell the blood of an ecosystem.

WHAT SHOULD I DO NEXT?

Be wary of new creatures. Even the inconspicuous bugs may be foreign invaders from another country. If you break out in bites or boils, take a sample of the organism and call the hospital – if you can reach the phone in time before paralysis and rigor mortis set in.

---

1. *See* Food chain collapse (92) • 2. Australia's rabbit problem can be blamed on 1 man and 24 rabbits. In 1859, Thomas Austin released the non-indigenous rabbits into the wild for his shooting hobby. Ten years later the population had rocketed to over 2 million rabbits • 3. Even though they may be aliens – *see* Space dust (244)

five magic beans from the stranger down the road in exchange for the family cow. Let's hope that golden-egg-laying geese are introduced to these regions soon.

VII

Fc

Food chain collapse

(92)

Food chain collapse. *phood··chayn··col·aps* – when Earth's once abundant creatures begin to disappear, one by one.

The killer whale is the ocean's top predator. It'll eat pretty much anything that's on the menu. A typical day may start with penguin with a hint of krill, followed by basking shark engorged with sperm whale and for dessert, dolphin blow-hole in oily squid ink.

The killer whale cares little for the insignificant, almost invisible beasties that cloud its view when hunting, but if it wasn't for these insignificant creatures then this top predator would disappear. Take krill and pteropod[1] out of the food chain equation, and fish without their micro diet will equal total marine food chain collapse.[2]

Over time

the whale's hors d'œuvres will start to disappear from the seafood menu, closely followed by the main courses, which in turn will force the whale to try the other strange-looking things on the menu as you should never swim on an empty stomach.[3]

---

1. Mini sea snails • 2. The years of pollution pumped into the oceans and warming seas are beginning to halt the development of the tiny sea creatures • 3. No bombing or heavy petting either • 4. Not the fish-eating kind • 5. *See* Pollination crisis (96)

The collapse is affecting the creatures of our green and pleasant lands, too. Snuff out the annoying flies, bees and wasps that get trapped inside your house and you may be inadvertently contributing to a new cycle of extinctions, from annoyingly b u z z i n g insects all the way up to bigger, tastier birds and beasts.

Maybe it's time for the carnivores to take a leaf out the vegetarians' book,[4] although the plants are suffering from a possible collapse too.[5] Just one more dead fly trapped in your badly fitted double glazing might be the tipping point for our very own eventual extinction.

WHEN WILL IT HAPPEN?

Sea stocks are estimated to be gone by 2050. There aren't plenty more fish in the sea.

WHAT SHOULD I LOOK FOR?

All sea creatures great and small.

WHEN SHOULD I START TO PANIC?

LATER · TOO LATE · SOON · NOW

PROBABILITY IT WILL HAPPEN?

High. Fish on Friday may be off the menu.

PROVERB CORNER

I know an old woman who swallowed a fly, I don't know why she swallowed a fly, perhaps we'll all die.

---

i. Sea snails • ii. Krill • iii. Small fish • iv. Squid • v. Large fish • vi. Penguins • vii. Birds • viii. Crabs
ix. Lobsters • x. Octopuses • xi. Turtles • xii. Sea lions • xiii. Emperor penguins • xiv. Dolphins
xv. Giant squid • xvi. Sperm whales • xvii. Blue whales • xviii. Sharks • xix. Plastic • xx. Killer whales

VII

Af

Animal
flatulence
(94)

Animal flatulence. *an·e·mal··flat·chew·lance* – it wasn't me, it was
the dog.

Expelling waste air is a necessity for all living creatures, and for some
people, it's also a pleasant pastime. But if you think you're a big polluter,
compared to the loveable tasty[1] cow, you're a lightweight.

  On its own, a cow is pretty harmless,[2] but as part of a gang, they're a
force to be reckoned with. There are over a billion of them out there, and
cows produce around three-quarters of all the methane that is emitted by
the world's creatures put together. Some would say that's showing off but
if you're in control of four methane-producing stomachs, you'd happily
break some mean wind to put the rest of us in our place,[3] especially as it's

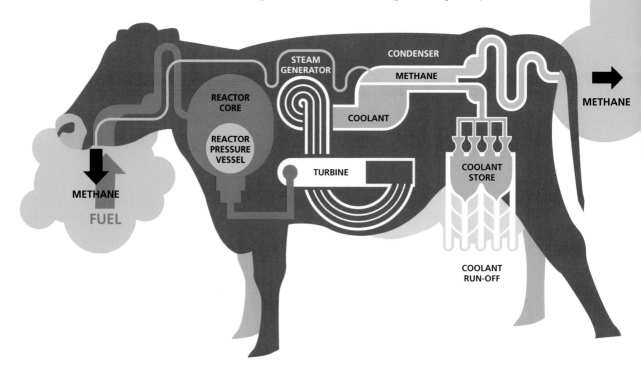

---

1. Add salt to taste • 2. Unless it's a jealous man-cow and he's seen you lock eyes with his bit of beef
on the side • 3. Check out YouChewb for cows setting light to their own farts

hard enough surpressing one gassy stomach let alone four. Each bovine is equipped with a complex system of tubes, pipes and valves that lead to a series of stomachs that process, condense, coagulate and churn the broken-down chemicals from their fodder and turn them into smog-inducing volatile organic compounds (VOCs).

Most of the cows' methane emissions are emitted via cow-sized belches when they eat, but combined with their farting these smog monsters are a potent force. They pollute the air we breathe with their foul stench, and their massive emissions go on to accelerate climate change, which we'd rather do without, even if they are making their donations for free. But we can't give the cows all the credit as we contribute too: sheep, pigs, goats, you, your momma, you name it – we're all doing our 'bit' to make our lovely fresh spring air smell a little bit staler.

WHEN WILL IT HAPPEN?

Animals are at it 24/7/365 and the air you breathe is heavy with animal eructation and turgidness. I'm sure you can smell a rat ... and cats, dogs, pigs, horses, etc. ...

WHAT SHOULD I LOOK FOR?

Heavy smog clinging to the farmers' fields throughout the day.

Bad smells when you're in the company of animals. The animal with the guilty face will be the culprit.

WHEN SHOULD I START TO PANIC?

Kangaroos don't emit methane due to bacteria inside their gut; so cows could be modified[4] to carry the bacteria, making methane gas a thing of the past, either that or we could fit animals with methane-collecting suits. Not very practical.

ME THANE, YOU THANE, WE THANE

4: The number of stomachs a cow has.
23: The amount of times methane is more harmful than CO_2.
280: The amount of methane a single cow can produce in a day in litres, although estimates swing from as low as 100 litres to 500 litres per day.
1.5: The number of cows in the world, in billions ... and rising ...

WHAT SHOULD I DO NEXT?

Buy air freshener.

4. *See* Genetics (188)

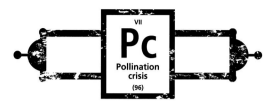

VII

Pc

Pollination crisis

(96)

Pollination crisis. *poll·in·a·chon··cry·sis* – when a plant hasn't got laid in quite a while.

Without pollination, plants couldn't reproduce. Some plants can self-pollinate but the vast majority rely on help from the yellow and black herb-crawlers that prostitute themselves around the garden. Bees crawl across the faces of the male plants attempting to plunder their nectar, the sweet sugars produced by flowers. As they bumble around the plant, the pollen attaches to their fur in the hope that, after the bee has finished its raid, the next plant it visits will be a female one. The plant is hoping that the little fluffer, loaded with its powdery reproductive spores, will transfer them, resulting in a flower bed of baby plants. It's believed that bees do the job of pollinating around a third of the crops that we rely on. So remove the bees, and the plants lying in their beds don't get laid and we don't eat.[1]

WHEN WILL IT HAPPEN?	WHEN SHOULD I START TO PANIC?	POLLINATION INVESTIGATION
Now. Bee numbers are already on the decline. In some parts of the world their numbers are way down.[2]		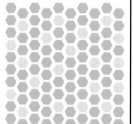
WHAT SHOULD I LOOK FOR?		
Bees. If your garden is beeless during the summer months then we're in trouble. Bees pollinate a wide variety of fruits and vegetables; they even pollinate cotton, so if you want to keep the shirt on your back, be nice to the bees.	If you like apples, kiwi fruit, strawberry, melon, green and red peppers, cashew nuts, cabbage, broccoli, green beans, runner beans, coffee, onion, pumpkin, courgettes and coconuts, amongst many others, start panicking now.	Insects pollinate 80% of crops, so let's hope that other pollinators such as wasps, butterflies, flies and midges don't follow the bees' lead and buzz off too. If this happens the entire world will have to share the remaining 20%.

Source: TEAGASC

1. And no more honey. With this decline no wonder bees spit in the honey just like a disgruntled waiter
2. The bees are in decline due to disease, lack of diversity and the loss of habitable homes

IN LOVING MEMORY
Que sera sera, It wasn't to bee, to bee

VII

Az

Animal zoonosis

(98)

Animal zoonosis. *ann·e·mal··zoo·know·sis* – when being sick as a parrot can, quite literally, be blamed on the birds.

Zoonosis, an animal version of a human epidemic, can destroy entire flocks of chickens and herds of cattle; it can ambush tigers, pigs can die in droves and it can murder crows. No animal is safe from infectious zoonoses, not even us. When a zoonosis crosses over the animal–human infection divide, it becomes an epidemic in human terms; man's best friend can become man's impounded worst enemy. Hanging out with any animal can be dangerous: an affectionate lick or a friendly bite from an infected beast can end up with you sweating like a pig. Birds can give you the flu, monkeys can pass on the pox and cows can make you go mad. If we're lucky, the disease will be confined to just one species, but more often, it spreads. One by one, different species of animal will become infected, leaving it difficult for us to know which animals we can trust, and the blame game starts. Prevention is better than cure and in many zoonosis cases, infected or suspected animals are herded together and invited to a farewell barbecue, but no one gets to eat these charred burgers. Keep a look-out for under-the-weather pets and farm animals, as we don't want to fall under their in-flu-ence with a new epidemic on our hands and hooves.

WHEN WILL IT HAPPEN?

Animals regularly get ill, it's only a matter of time before the animal kingdom sneezes and we catch their pox, flu, virus or whatever ...

SOME ILLNESSES TO LOOK OUT FOR

BSE,[1] SARS,[2] avian influenza,[3] swine flu and man flu amongst many others.

WHEN SHOULD I START TO PANIC?

LATER · TOO LATE · now · soon

Hotfoot and mouth it to the hospital if you have any unusual symptoms.

WHAT SHOULD I LOOK FOR?

Cows looking peaky, birds throwing up and ill asses taking days off.

WHAT SHOULD I DO NEXT?

Check your local health centre has vaccines in stock against animal zoonoses. This way you can flip the bird to avian influenza.

---

1. Bovine spongiform encephalopathy or mad cow disease • 2. Severe acute respiratory syndrome
3. Bird flu

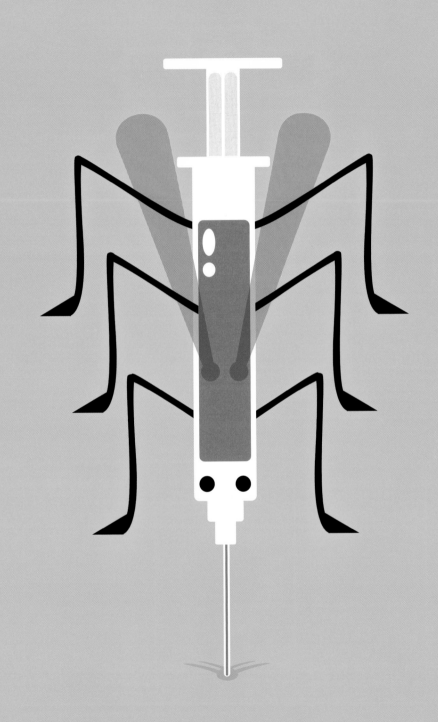

Over fishing. *oh·ver·fizh·shing* – when the fish have had their chips.

There was a time, billions of years ago, when all life lived in the sea. The place was packed to the gills with aquatic life but some of its scaly residents yearned for a vacation, causing some plucky fish to go and see what was beside the sea. These illegal immigrants to the land were the first to realise that they'd be better off staying in this brave new world, which led to the border being breached by more sea creatures seeking life up top. Billions of years later, the upright fish that we've become have perfected a system of helping the rest of our aquatic cousins to come and join us up here on the land, whether they like it or not.

Unfortunately for the fish that stayed in the ocean, they can swim but they can't hide from the massive nets that trawl the seas to hunt them down. No fish is safe from capture, as demand is out-stripping supply. Fish stocks are plummeting and they may reach a tipping point where certain species can't recover. Along with the 100 million tons of fish that are removed from the sea every year, other unwanted sea creatures – including the ocean's top predators – become tangled up in the nets and their numbers also suffer. Remove the kings of the sea and the next in line will take their place at the

WHEN WILL IT HAPPEN?

Stocks are falling now. It could be time to genetically modify fish to reproduce all year round.[1]

WHAT SHOULD I LOOK FOR?

Fish. If you can't see plenty of fish in the sea then put your rod away and let stocks recover.

WHEN SHOULD I START TO PANIC?

The fish have had their chips, as we need them to go with ours.

WHAT SHOULD I DO NEXT?

You could become a lacto-ovo-vegetarian and help save the fish and whales.[2] Becoming a pescatarian won't help, plus it's cheating. Pescatarianism isn't vegetarianism as vegetables have faces only if you arrange them correctly on your plate.[3]

---

1. *See* Genetic modification (190) • 2. *See* Food chain collapse (92) • 3. Potatoes have eyes and you can also have cauliflower ears

top, and they can be even more destructive than the previous kings. So whether they're destined for our stomachs, fish ponds or the trophy wall, the leftover fish will be left with a much bigger and less crowded pond. But it does beg the question: if you remove all the fish from the sea, will that counter the effects of rising sea levels?

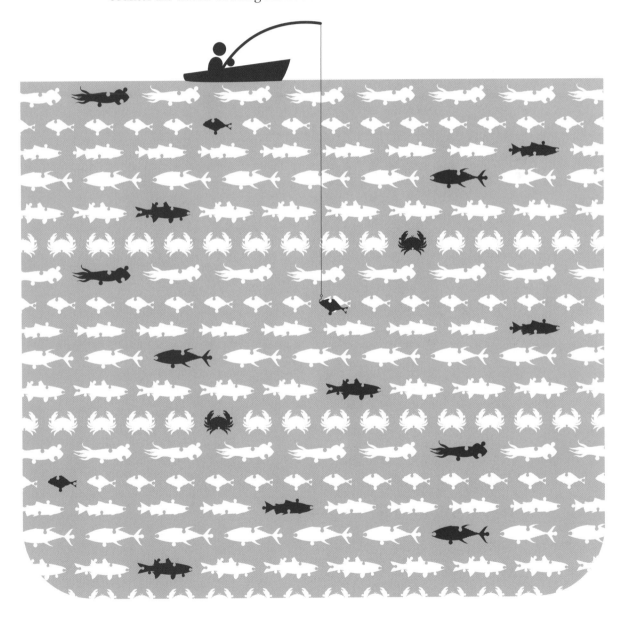

VIII

It's all your fault

It's all your fault *itz··all··yor··fallt* – when the Earth can sit back and wait for our self-inflicted fireworks.

There are natural events on this planet that could easily wipe the human race from existence, whereas other less instant events need a helping hand to be kickstarted into motion.

On their own they may not be able to assassinate us outright, but if they join forces with other environmental calamities then it could be enough to choke, cook, squeeze, drown or coax us into oblivion.

Humankind has a knack of putting itself in the line of fire unnecessarily, so by plundering the Earth's assets and destroying its natural resources we're sending the human race down a dead-end street. This could be the end of the road ...

_____

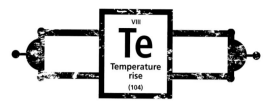

VIII
Te
Temperature
rise
(104)

Temperature rise. *tem·purr·ray·chure··ryze*–when the greenhouse we've built around ourselves starts to hot up and kills all the pretty flowers ... and the weeds.

When man started to industrially revolt in the middle of the nineteenth century, his actions left a long-lasting legacy. As we pumped the atmosphere with smoke, nobody gave a second thought to where the black clouds would go, but as if by magic, they became invisible within minutes. No one at that time realised that the disappearing clouds would reveal themselves to future generations and threaten their very existence.

The Earth and its atmosphere is like a meatball inside a sealed Tupperware tub that's been left in the sunlight far too long with nowhere for the heat to escape. After almost two centuries of us pumping nasty clouds into the environment, the temperature is climbing. Ice-cream salesmen will rejoice at this news but isn't great for everyone and everything else.

With even a slight rise in temperature, our Earth and all its inhabitants will have to get used to a hotter, unpredictable new world. Some species will cope just fine with the sudden temperature increase, others may even thrive, but the majority will suffer, struggle and die.

Glaciers will fall, the gulf stream will fail,[1] rain will sting,[2] cool places will become hotter, hot places will become unbearable and we're all in for a lot of stormy weather.

WHEN WILL IT HAPPEN?	**WHEN SHOULD I START TO PANIC?**	**WHAT SHOULD I LOOK FOR?**
It's predicted that the world's temperature will keep rising. If the polar regions melt they may cause the gulf stream to collapse. Others predict this may trigger a new ice age. Cold may become the new hot.	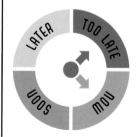	Key a look out for catastrophic end-of-the-world scenarios as far as the eye can see and beyond. A tiny change in the world's temperature will bring about all kinds of death and disaster.

1. *See* Gulf stream collapse (116) 2. *See* Acid rain (122)

VIII

Ws

Warming seas

(106)

Warming seas. *warming··seez* – when the oceans become hotter through global warming, causing coral grief.

With global temperature rise comes the inevitable warming of the seas: a bonus for surfers and English Channel swimmers, but not so great for the creatures that aren't used to soaking away the hours in a hot tub.

By deep ocean standards, the shallow tropical seas are already pretty warm, which is ideal for the fish that thrive there and the coral that supports them, but one effect of warming seas will be an impact on the coral.

Reefs are sensitive seacosystems, the coral of which have internal thermostats that turn off due to a sudden temperature rise or fall, triggering a chain of events that can upset the underwater seacosystem and can destroy an entire reef. These temperature shocks can be triggered by El Niño[1] events, which cause the reefs to bleach and marine seacosystems to be dropped into a lot of hot water.

Coral, the king and queen[2] of the reef, gets along with most[3] marine organisms within its kingdom. But when it becomes stressed, getting too hot under the coral, it takes it heat out on the algae that accompanies it. The algae are banished from the coral inner sanctum causing the reef to become less vibrant. This in turn starves the seacosystem of life. Look

WHEN WILL IT HAPPEN?

The bath water is getting hotter and the sponges are feeling the squeeze, they've taken on as much as they can.

WHAT SHOULD I LOOK FOR?

Unusual exotic fish or tropical sea creatures that are new to your coastline.

WHEN SHOULD I START TO PANIC?

Temperature rise affects the majority of the ocean not a drop in the ocean.

WHAT WILL HAPPEN NEXT?

The hot sea bath may soon be turned into an ocean jacuzzi if the methane trapped under the cold seabed is heated up to a temperature that could cause it to be released into the atmosphere,[4] causing global temperatures to accelerate even faster and further.

---

1. The 1998 El Niño event was extra strong as a result of climate change, which caused the reefs to bleach further – *see* El Niño and La Niña (58) • 2. Or 'Quing' or 'Keen', as some coral are hermaphroditic or asexual • 3. Although the crown-of-thorns starfish snack on coral. Their population is booming and they have few natural predators • 4. *See* Methane sink (78)

after your algae, otherwise it may be the death of you. Life may return to the reef one day or it may move on for ever, causing the reef to fully die out. In twenty years time' there may be nothing left atoll.

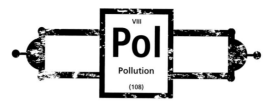

VIII
Pol
Pollution
(108)

Pollution. *pol·loo·chon·* – when the air you breathe is impure.

History has given us many lessons in pollution. When the Victorians invented the smoke factories of the Industrial Revolution, little thought was given to their effects on the environment. The smoke by-product was belched out of the factories into the air. The Victorians hadn't realised that the smoke would come back to haunt them. It joined forces with its airborne friend, called fog. Between them, this formidable team produced smog[1] and blinded the residents of the major industrial cities time and time again for years to come. At around the same time as the thick pea-soup fogs, London stank. Anything that could be flushed away was, which then ran into the Thames. Everything made its way to the river: industrial overflow, dead bodies, blood, chemicals and human waste, including many microscopic nasties.[2] Following years of misuse, the summer of 1858 was a scorcher and bacteria thrived in the river, causing the big stink.

If you were unlucky enough to live in London at this time, you couldn't see anything and you didn't dare breathe in. Not only that, the pollution had worked its way into the soil so that the root vegetables that were eaten contained essence of death from the air and water. That said, at least the human waste made the vegetables grow bigger. Lessons have been learned, but particulates are still building up in the atmosphere, using the healthy clouds as hosts, with the intention of raining down their polluted cargo[3] into your skyward-looking eyes.

WHEN WILL IT HAPPEN?

Now, as everything is polluted, the air, the sea, the soil, rivers, lakes and, ultimately, the food on your plate. Light pollution confuses the birds and noise pollution inhibits sleep.

Pollution hates you.

WHEN SHOULD I START TO PANIC?

HOW DO I FIND POLLUTION?

You may have found pollution, even if you can't see it. If your drinking water tastes funny, looks brown or tinted, if the sea is oily, you can see naked trees or if your vegetables are on the small side.

---

1. Originally named 'foke', it was changed to 'smog' due to foke's similarity to 'folk' and 'fuck' • 2. This was also drinking water for some • 3. *See* Acid rain (122)

Ozone depletion. *oh·zone··dee·plee·shon* – when the protective ozone layer starts to leak.

Just like a superhero deciding whether to use his powers for good or bad, ozone has the same choice, but it can't quite decide whose side it's on.

Born of the very substance that can ultimately kill it, ozone repels the daily onslaught of harmful ultraviolet rays from the evil Sun that rain down a whole world of cosmic terror on the Earth. Ozone has formed a defensive layer around the Earth, 15 miles above our heads, which absorbs the evil rays, keeping the citizens of the Earth protected. But although ozone saves our lives, the closer it gets to the Earth, the more harmful it becomes. Ozone is a pollutant and can't mix with the rest of us. Becoming a social outcast, it walks a fine line between saving us and destroying us, and for all its help, humankind tried to destroy it with machines by replicating the Arctic's freezing conditions within our own kitchens.[1] Ironically, while the cold was coming into our homes, the hot gases that were released headed outwards, making the world a much warmer place and destroying ozone in the process. Happily a truce was called and humankind has acknowledged the significant contributions that ozone has made to our lives. We can all sleep soundly in our beds thanks to ozone.

WHEN WILL IT HAPPEN?

Now. We have to help ozone as it's depleting due to the pollution we've already created and the toll of the rays it defends us from.

WHAT SHOULD I LOOK FOR?

An invisible superhero that spreads itself thinly and is rarely seen.

WHEN SHOULD I START TO PANIC?

We've already helped[2] but we can do more by turning the air-con down.

WHAT SHOULD I DO NEXT?

We need to help ozone in its fight against cosmic evil.

By swapping your Arctic ice replicators[1] for upgrades that don't emit harmful ozone gases, you will be able to help our protector who'll thwart the Sun and his evil ultraviolet ray ways.

---

1. Also known as 'refrigerators' • 2. By phasing out the CFC-making machines.[2] Now they've been phased out the layer is getting better

VIII

Ff

Fossil fuels

(112)

Fossil fuels. *ffoss·ill··ffewlls* – the non-renewable natural resources of oil, coal and natural gas that we love to burn.

It took the Earth millions of years to form the pools of gas, oil and coal that we discovered hidden inside Earth's deep pockets alongside all the other fossils and sweet wrappers; it's only taking us centuries to burn it all up. We're consuming these fossil fuels as fast as a gang of school kids in an unsupervised candy store guzzling sweets and just like Spangles,[1] the non-renewable fossil fuels are no longer in production.[2] With this constant plundering and with no time to renew them within anyone's lifetime, they'll completely run out, leaving us to find new and inventive uses for our obsolete cars.

It is estimated that there is enough of these fuels to see us up to about 2050 but it's already having an immediate impact: oil prices are volatile, as are your household bills, and if you're unlucky enough to live in a country that relies on another nation to intravenously feed it with gas then just make sure your country stays on speaking terms with the big gas daddies.[3] Predicting how much of these resources we have left is notoriously hard; one day the intravenous drips will stop dropping, just like that. The days of cheap oil, gas and coal are over; the end of fossil fuels has just begun.

WHEN WILL IT HAPPEN?

Sooner than you think. Ditch the car as walking is the new driving. Start building a wind farm on your driveway asap.

WHAT SHOULD I LOOK FOR?

All your favourite things becoming defunct: cars, petrol, planes, gas fires, plastic, etc.

WHEN SHOULD I START TO PANIC?

LATER · TOO LATE · NOW · SOON

Unless you've got time to wait millions of years for the next batches of fuel.

WHAT SHOULD I DO NEXT?

Stop using the limited fossil fuels and start relying different kinds of power as burning the last drop of fuel and rock will ultimately cook the planet.

Try digging mile-deep holes in your garden to harness the free geothermal energy to power your home.

---

1. Square boiled sweets from the past, in various flavours all featuring a bad 70s font called 'bell bottom'; how we miss them • 2. Not in a short time scale sense • 3. Like Russia, *see* World leaders (170)

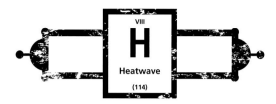

VIII

H

Heatwave

(114)

Heatwave. *heet·wayv* – when the world's temperature begins to race, ultimately leaving no clear winners, just a dead heat.

With the world's temperature running higher and higher, the hottest-day records are continually being broken, and global warming contributes to more record-breaking medals year after year.

A heatwave that follows the anticipointment[1] of a potentially hot summer turning into a wash-out is greeted with bare chests and bodies spread across every free piece of grass or sand as far as the eye can see, but in record-breaking years, the heat proves too much to bare all. The world's average temperature is rising as fast as the protection factor on sun-creams; although in 2003 the creams didn't help, as the heat claimed over 20,000 Europeans' lives prematurely. Not only do we have to look after ourselves during a heatwave: the livestock feel the heat, too, and they can't nip to the fridge for an ice-cold beer or take a cooling shower at will. We don't want them to die before we want them to. Hotter summers and milder winters also create the perfect conditions for annoying flies and diseases to thrive, and in the colder parts glaciers will melt quicker, triggering avalanches if, at this point, there is any snow left to launch. We may look forward to the summer but it turns out the heat isn't so cool after all.

WHEN WILL IT HAPPEN?	**WHEN SHOULD I START TO PANIC?**	**WHAT SHOULD I DO NEXT?**
If you can't stand the heat get out of the bitchin' as it's our own fault.		Don't just prepare for the heat as it can bring with it some very stormy weather.
All you can do is roll with it and hope the heat doesn't have your number.		Stock up on tinned food and water in case of crop failure and drought, make sure your home insurance covers flash floods and have enough fly swatters for those pesky flies.
WHAT SHOULD I LOOK FOR?	The human flowers in the worldwide greenhouse will soon be wilting.	
Shade.		

1. *See* Glossary (263)

VIII

Gs

Gulf stream
collapse

(116)

Gulf stream collapse. *gulf··stream··col·aps* – when the Earth's hot taps are turned off.

The gulf stream is one part of a fast-flowing system of warm and cold currents that circulate around the globe. Cold water in the Pacific Ocean is heated up where it begins to flow. The warm water travels near to the surface of the oceans. As it holidays around the seas, it heats up the waters of the Pacific islands, Australia and South Africa, whilst at the same time evaporating and becoming denser due to the increasing salt content. The water continues north through the Atlantic Ocean, it gets pushed through the Gulf of Mexico, it then travels north beyond the British Isles. This water is so warm that it actually heats the climate of Europe by about 9°C. The gulf stream finally reaches the colder, denser and saltier waters of the Arctic Circle. The heavier water is then pushed down to the ocean floor and along the depths of the ocean, back from whence it came, starting the cycle all over again. It's wonderful when it works, as Northern Europe would be difficult to live in without it. Its collapse will cause world temperatures to plummet, the Arctic ice will spread covering large parts of North America and Eurasia, triggering a full-scale premature ice age that will occur within years rather than decades.[1] Still waters freeze deep.

HOW CAN IT HAPPEN?

Through a rise in temperature or a sudden injection of fresh water.[2]

The oceans are already showing signs of warming and Greenland's glaciers are releasing fresh water.

Maybe it's time to retire to warmer climes like Spain or further south, just to be sure.

WHEN SHOULD I START TO PANIC?

It's getting warmer, which means it could soon be getting much colder.

WHAT SHOULD I LOOK FOR?

The seas warming by a few more degrees than normal. Glaciers reducing in size and diluting the oceans, making the water colder still. Also look for cold and still stagnant seas and a big white walkway that connects all the northern hemisphere continents.

---

1. Although this theory is a controversial one and climate change may offset some of the cooling. A weakened gulf stream could dramatically alter tropical rainfall patterns, raising the North Atlantic sea level – *see* Rising sea levels (118) • 2. *See* Melting glaciers (70)

Ocean Conveyor

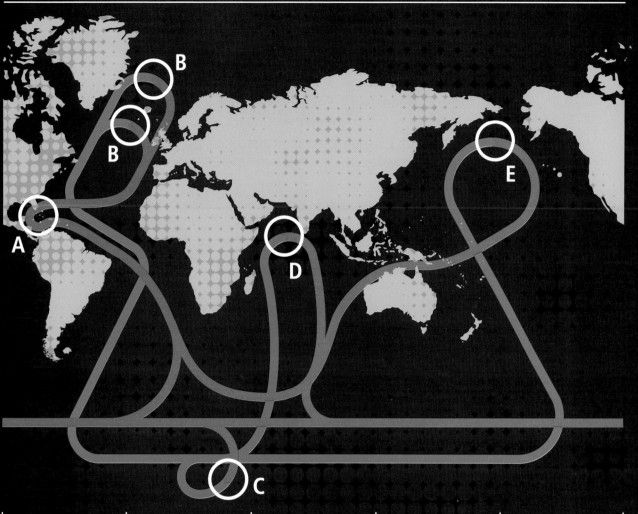

A. The Gulf Stream

Possible service disruption

B. North Atlantic Drift

Good service

C. Antarctic Ocean

Good service

D. Indian Ocean

Good service

E. Pacific Ocean

Good service

VIII
Rs
Rising sea levels
(118)

Rising sea levels. *ry·sing··see··lev·alls* – when the frozen water of the world turns to liquid and wellies become your everyday shoes.

The sea levels of the Earth rise and fall depending on how much of the world's fresh water is locked up in glaciers or ice caps; not only that, but the sea also expands when it warms up.[1] With an ice age, the sea level falls, whereas the opposite is true in a period of intense warming. Although we're currently in an ice epoch,[2] our contributions to global warming are causing the glaciers of the world to retreat, leaving a whole pile of water where the frozen stuff used to be, so the ice is melting sooner than was anticipated. The meniscus of the land is about to be breached and if all the ice melts it is guestimated that a sea level rise of 1 metre would cause 17% of Bangladesh to become a modern-day Atlantis, islands like the Maldives would disappear and low-lying cities such as London, New York and Amsterdam would become like aquarium model cities in a worldwide fish bowl.

WHEN WILL IT HAPPEN?

Right now. Blue is the new white. If you can easily see a polar bear or an animal with a name starting with 'snow' then we're in real trouble.

WHAT SHOULD I LOOK FOR?

Keep an eye out for the wet, blue wobbly stuff that comes out of your taps creeping up your garden path if you're lucky. If you're unlucky it'll be a wall of dirty brown water instead.

WHEN SHOULD I START TO PANIC?

Every teeny tiny drop of fresh water that is added to the ocean is raising the water levels bit by bit, so when the sea throws a wobbly on the land, make sure your dinghy is fully inflated.

POSSIBILITY IT WILL HAPPEN?

Around 1 in 2 of the world's population live within 60 km of the coast, so live further inland or make sure you can swim, as you could be swimming up your high street soon …

Source: ICM

1. *See* Warming seas (106) • 2. *See* Ice age (68)

EARTH **2150**

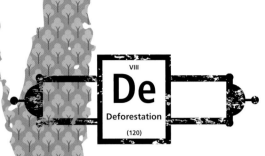

De

VIII

Deforestation

(120)

Deforestation. *dee·four·res·tay·chon* – **when the world's lungs are dissected and made into coffee tables.**

The world used to be much greener than it is today. At one point, half of the USA was forest, England was an even greener and pleasanter land and Greenland really did live up to its name.[1]

Deforestation has been happening for millennia. Farming domestic animals in a forest is impossible, so the unwanted trees were removed, making more room for grazing. Next, the trees that were needed to keep the fire alive were removed, then the trees that burnt down when the fire got out of control went; next went the trees that built the houses and the boats, etc. This has resulted in deforestation on a global scale, and now all that remains of the large ancient forests are the few tropical rainforests of the world and they're shrinking too.

WHEN WILL IT HAPPEN?

Every day large parts of the world's rainforests are going missing.

WHAT SHOULD I LOOK FOR?

Holes where bits of the rainforest used to be. Wildlife leaving the forests and setting up home in your garden, making it look like an over-subscribed zoo.

Check eBay for the missing wood. If you see a sideboard that looks like it should belong in a rainforest, buy it and send it home.

WHEN SHOULD I START TO PANIC?

LATER / TOO LATE / SOON / NOW

Less forest means more carbon dioxide for our atmosphere and our lungs.

Easter Island used to be covered in trees, and look what happened to its population. No wonder the stone statues look so sad.

FOREST COVERAGE AND SPECIES (%)

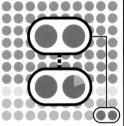

- 70% of the Earth is water
- 30% of the Earth is land,
- 10% of which is desert
- and just 2% of the Earth is rainforest
- Up to 90% of Earth's species live in the rainforest

WHAT SHOULD I DO NEXT?

Let the forest reign.

Source: Rainforest information centre/Rainforest Foundation

1. Although Greenland would have been deforested by the climate we can't blame humans for that one
2. *See* Carbon sink (76) • 3. *See* Extinction (6)

The world's rainforests remove tons of the harmful gases in our bad stale air and replace them with fresh air through photosynthesis, helping the forest to grow and helping us to breathe.[2] But while the trees are giving us the kiss of life, we're performing back-street surgery on them. It seems money only grows on chopped-down trees.

Unauthorised logging in the rainforest is like removing the good lung of a smoker and leaving behind the bad one, which will eventually collapse too. Every tree removed impacts on the ecosystem, which ultimately impacts on us. There are thousands of undiscovered species that'll be made extinct through logging even before they've been logged[3] and as in previous millennia, the rainforests are being cleared to make way for livestock to graze and also for cocaine plantations, amongst many other things. All this destruction could even go so far as to create new climate conditions, resulting in the wooded areas being renamed droughtforests.

So drugs and food are taking priority over breathing, and the weather systems will suffer too; at least the atmospheric pressure can still get high.

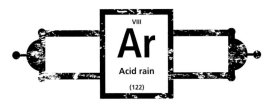

VIII

Ar

Acid rain

(122)

Acid rain. *ass·id··reign* – when raindrops keep falling on your head, burn your eyes out and cause teardrops of blood.

Long ago in the Emerald Isle, a unanimous decision made by the leprechaun community saw them adopt a foolproof banking system that has foiled would-be raiders for centuries. The decision to keep their pots of gold at the end of rainbows was inspired; not only can no one find the end of the rainbow but rainbows don't need pin numbers or passwords. The leprechauns have had centuries of trouble-free banking and even in the age of acid rain, their hauls are still safe as houses: gold doesn't corrode.[1]

Rain becomes high in acid when mixing with fossil fuel emissions from industry or transport; it also forms through wildfires and volcanoes. This substance abuse alters the water, making raindrops totally loaded on acid.

When the tanked-up raindrops fall to the ground and mix with soils, ponds and rivers, they inflict their chemical abuse on the living organisms they come into contact with. Acid rain strips the bark off trees so that they become even more at one with nature than they are already, and it's known for fish to become so full to the gills that they swim upside down. So be careful next time you're catching snowflakes on your tongue: some of them may burn.

WHEN WILL IT HAPPEN?

Now. Our pollution is pumped up into the atmosphere, as it has to end up somewhere, gravity makes sure our rubbish gets returned.

WHAT SHOULD I LOOK FOR?

Lifeless lakes, upside-down fish and uninhibited naked trees.

WHEN SHOULD I START TO PANIC?

When you're looking to the skies, use eye protection.

HERE COMES THE ACID RAIN AGAIN

Humans can generate acid rain in many ways with such things as cars, industry and nuclear war, and Mother Nature can generate it too via asteroid strikes, volcanic eruptions and wildfires. Acid rain can also fall as acid snow and hail. Acid fog and mist can occur too.

---

1. Gold doesn't corrode but it does tarnish. When you're hunting for the leprechauns' pot of gold at the end of a rainbow, try looking for a pot of green instead. Once found, some polishing may be necessary.

VIII
Abc
Atmospheric
brown cloud
(124)

Atmospheric brown cloud. *at·moss·fair·rick··brr·owyn··klowd* – the dirty hue hanging around developing countries.

For a century and a half, the Western world has belched smoke from every chimney possible without a second thought. The consequences became apparent just as the ecological time bomb exploded in our faces. Although it's too little, too late, the developed world is slowly making inroads to turn the Industrial Revolution from revolting evolution into a green revolution,[1] just as the developing world's own industrial revolution is evolving into an atmospheric brown one. Countries including India and China have lagged far behind the Western world in industry but they're more than making up for it now.

Western countries are still the biggest polluters,[2] but East Asia has a nasty stain on its hands, in its eyes and all over its hair in the form of the already present atmospheric brown cloud[3] that currently sits over it. This brown fog has been developing for years. India and China, amongst others, are developing so fast that by the time all their coal-fired power stations are built, it would be no surprise if there were no more coal left in the world to power them, as they seem to be building so many.[4]

During the monsoon season the cloud hangs in the air like a bad brown smell, and it has even been blamed for the lack of rainfall in other parts of the world, including Australia. So how do you get rid of it? The answer's simple: cut emissions. It should be as easy as ABC.

WHEN WILL IT HAPPEN?	**WHEN SHOULD I START TO PANIC?**	**WHAT WILL HAPPEN NEXT?**
It'll get into the water through rain, and poison the fish in the rivers, lakes and seas. Look for clear skies, as you're not going to see the sunshine through the pollution otherwise.		The heat that the cloud traps underneath it will help to accelerate the melting of the Himalayan glaciers, which can cause floods, then drought in the regions below the mountains.

1. Very, very slowly • 2. The average European consumes six times as much of the Earth's resources as an average Indian person or three times as much as an average Chinese person • 3. Formerly known as the 'Asian brown cloud' until India complained • 4. It is believed that China is opening two coal-fired power stations a week

Cs
VIII
Chemical sink
(126)

Chemical sink. *kem·michael··synk* – when the chemicals in your toilet make a lavatory of the Arctic.

The Arctic region looks pristine and white, but you'd be mistaken if you thought it was all to do with the snow lying around, as some of it could be down to bleach. It has been discovered that the Arctic contains harmful chemicals. Hidden inside the frozen ice are chemicals that have been deposited in the area over the years by water and air that's travelled from all four corners of the globe.[1] Once the pollution reaches the Arctic it can be trapped inside the ice for many years until it's released back to the sea as the ice melts. These chemicals find their way back into the ocean, into the fish and into the food chain. But the chemicals have been known to enter the food chain at a much earlier stage. It's been discovered that sperm whales contain high amounts of flame retardant, perfect in a wildfire situation but not applicable in an environment where fires are highly improbable, but not impossible;[2] and, ironically, polar bears have been found to contain chemicals that are used for coolant. These chemicals have health implications for the entire food chain as they've also found inside us.[3] If the fact that the substances are already in our systems doesn't compound the situation, then what will?

WHEN WILL IT HAPPEN?

24/7/365. It occurs every time pollution is pumped into the air and sea or dumped on the land.

WHAT SHOULD I LOOK FOR?

Polar bears that aren't hot, whales that aren't on fire, sea birds shrink-wrapped on the inside.

WHEN SHOULD I START TO PANIC?

If you like your meat organic then don't eat polar beasts.

WHAT SHOULD I DO NEXT?

Put the flame-retardant animals to good use by pitting nature against nature, it's the last thing a wildfire will expect.

The polar bears can clear the route while the whales can utilise their onboard water-ejecting system to douse the flames.

---

1. But mainly North America and Europe • 2. *See* Methane sink (78) • 3. The same chemicals have been found in human milk

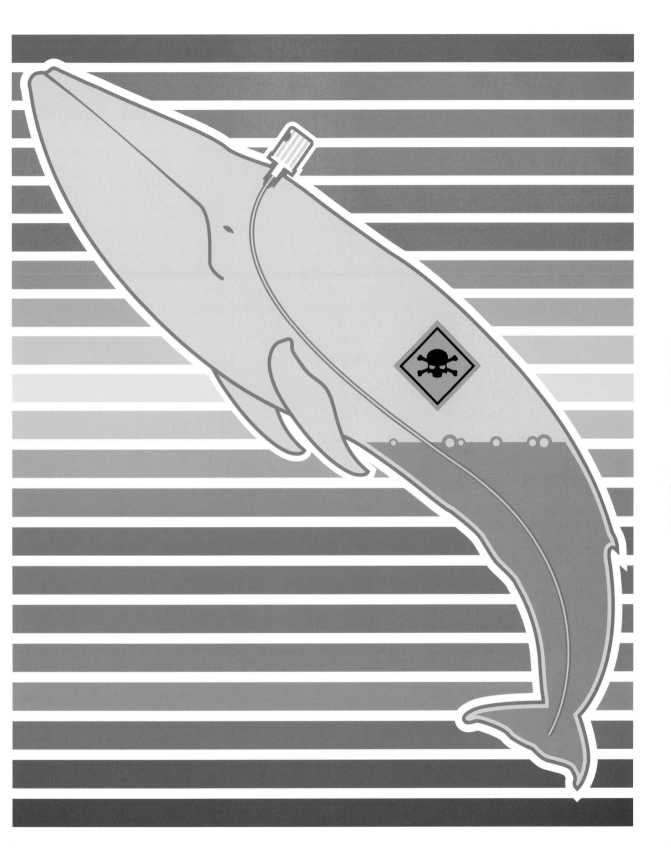

VIII

Ov

Over population

(128)

Over population. *oh·ver·pop·you·lay·chon* – more and more people on our smaller and smaller planet.

We humans are multiplying like a disease.[1] In 1804 we became 1 billion people. It had taken 250,000 years to reach the 1 billion milestone but then it only took another 123 years to reach 2 billion in 1927. Then the records kept tumbling In 1960, we became 3 billion (after 33 years), 4 billion in 1974 (after 14 years), 5 billion in 1987 (after 13 years) and in 1999 we reached 6 billion (after 12 years). So where does this leave us? It leaves us with a hell of a lot of mouths to feed and with less and less space to cultivate the land to feed them.[2] Not only that, with 250 births and only 103 deaths every minute, we have an extra 211,680 people to feed every day, which gives new meaning to the term 'baby boom'.

WHEN WILL IT HAPPEN?

The world is already over populated and it's going to get worse but by using contraception, women waiting later in life to start having children and China's one child policy, the world's population growth shouldn't rise as fast as it used to, at least for a bit.

WHAT SHOULD I LOOK FOR?

People everywhere you look. The feeling of never being alone. Queues everywhere.

WHEN SHOULD I START TO PANIC?

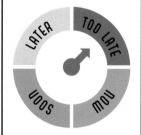

In 2012 the population of the world will reach 7bn (13 years from 6bn). We're due to reach 8bn by 2025 (13 years from 7bn) and 9 billion by 2040 (15 years since 8bn). More people means a lot more babies. You're never going to feel lonely again.

WHERE ON EARTH IS EVERYONE? (%)

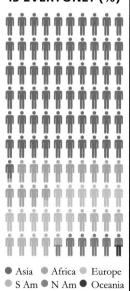

● Asia ● Africa ● Europe
● S Am ● N Am ● Oceania

Source: UN

---

1. And the only cure is total annihilation • 2. An average European consumes six times as much of the Earth's resources as an average Indian or three times as much as an average Chinese

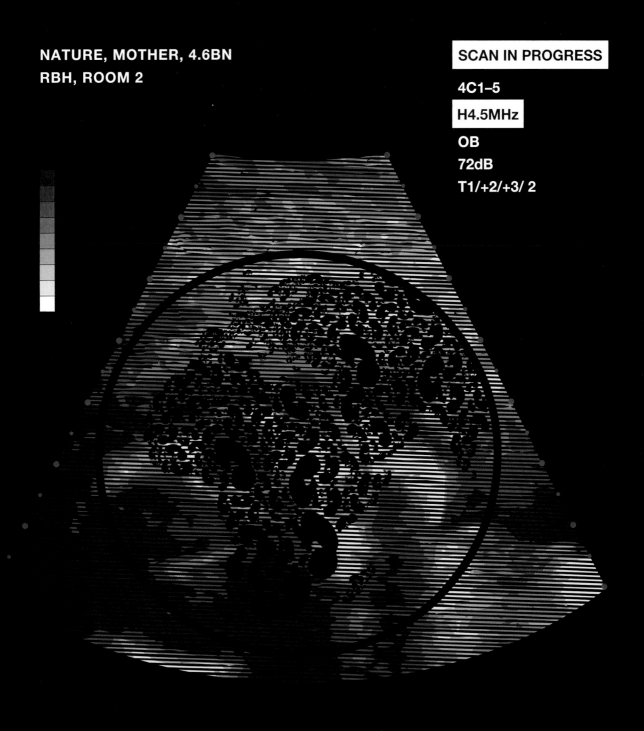

NATURE, MOTHER, 4.6BN
RBH, ROOM 2

SCAN IN PROGRESS

4C1–5

H4.5MHz

OB

72dB

T1/+2/+3/ 2

250 BABIES PER MIN
51% M – 49% F

16 MAR 09
17:35:09 PM

Sp

VIII

Space issues

(130)

Space issues. *spayse··ish·uze* – when there's no room left at the inn, in the stable, in the field or anywhere on the face of the planet.

An over-populated planet[1] comes with a whole world of space issues. Not only do we have to find space for over 6 billion people to reside in, we also have to feed these hungry mouths with billions of acres of crops, not to mention the space we need for our livestock: they take up a lot of grazing room before we can chow down on their tasty asses. We also need to find space for the dying, as 103 souls elbow their way into Heaven or squeeze themselves into Hell every sixty seconds. Luckily, we can cremate them, just like we accidentally cremate the meat on our unattended barbecue.[2] But industrious world residents are finding various new ways to make space for our needs. Greenfield sites are being viewed with envious eyes, and in the Amazon rainforest, ranchers are illegally creating space for their livestock by removing the unhelpful trees.[3] These days there is also less room to sit due to a recent obesity epidemic resulting in everything having to be made wider for the larger proportion of our global community.[4] But maybe we can put the enormous trash vortex we're inadvertently making in the Pacific Ocean to good use, by digging ourselves out of one big overcrowded hole and getting ourselves into another plastic and soggy kettle of fish.[5]

WHEN WILL IT HAPPEN?	**WHEN SHOULD I START TO PANIC?**	**WHAT SHOULD I DO NEXT?**

<table>
<tr>
<td>It's a small world that gets a lot smaller by 49 extra people every 20 seconds.

WHAT SHOULD I LOOK FOR?

Look for any available space that hasn't been developed yet. Alas, paradise may have already been paved over.</td>
<td>

There's nothing you can do about it except promote contraception.</td>
<td>The world's population is set to reach 9 billion by 2040, so we really should start looking into acquiring land that no one has yet laid claim to. The Moon and Mars are next in line for development as there's so little space left down here and there's plenty of space out there.</td>
</tr>
</table>

1. *See* Over population (128) • 2. Do not attempt to cremate your dead on a barbecue, seek professional help, unless you're a murderer then you're on your own • 3. *See* Deforestation (120) • 4. *See* Obesity (138) • 5. *See* Plastic soup (132)

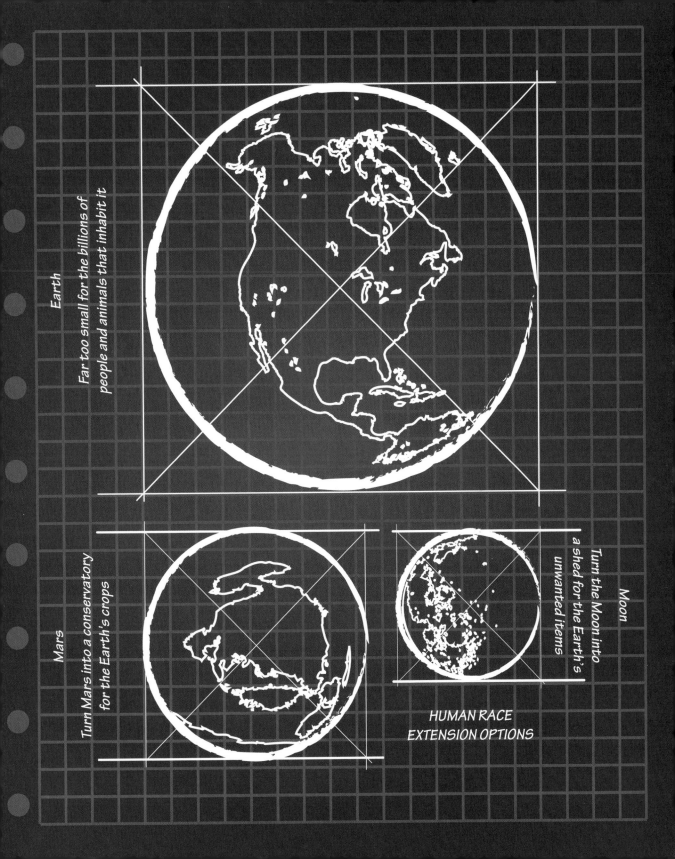

Earth

Far too small for the billions of people and animals that inhabit it

Mars

Turn Mars into a conservatory for the Earth's crops

Moon

Turn the Moon into a shed for the Earth's unwanted items

HUMAN RACE
EXTENSION OPTIONS

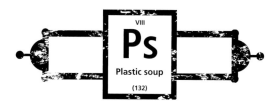

VIII

Ps

Plastic soup

(132)

Plastic soup. *pla·stick··supe* – a toxic-tasting salty sea broth of toothbrushes, bottles and bags that the sea creatures believe are tasty colourful snacks.

The sea is the keeper of many dark secrets, and legend has it that there are actually nine continents in the world: there are two more islands named East and West Garbagia. If you check your atlas you'll find no mention of these mysterious worlds. Few have seen these hidden continents and lived to tell the tale. The stories tell of unreachable lands, made from neither rock nor soil, just under the surface of the water.

To find Garbagia, set sail for the North Pacific. The Eastern patch is to the right of Japan; look above Hawaii for the West.

These 'lands' reveal themselves only to those sailors who traverse these unusual waters. Sat-nav is useless, as the satellites cannot pick out these low-lying 'lands'; they appear only to a sea-faring few. So what do the new worlds promise? Well, that's the problem, when you find them they're really rubbish. These new worlds are man-made; they've formed in an area known as the North Pacific gyre. This region features rotating ocean currents that swirl in circles to create a dead zone at the centre, where the non-biodegradable trash churns. You can find everything in this soggy jumble but it's not getting any smaller: at present the two worlds combined are as large as the entire United States of America.[1] So with these two huge discoveries it's time to throw away the old history books and rewrite them, as long as the old books don't find their way into the sea.

WHAT SHOULD I LOOK FOR?	**WHEN SHOULD I START TO PANIC?**	**WHAT SHOULD I DO NEXT?**
A whole world of plastic under your boat's feet. Try fishing and see if you can catch live fish-flavoured aquatic vertebrates rather than the dead strawberry-flavoured condoms you are bound to catch.		We should remove every single ton. If we did succeed in removing it all from the world's oceans, would this mean that the sea levels would drop, thus postponing the effects of sea rise?

---

1. Maybe not Alaska, but who counts that as the USA anyway?

East and
West Garbagia

VIII

Pn

Pandemic

(134)

Pandemic. *pan·dem·mick* – when an epidemic outbreak turns from epidemonium into pandemonium.

A pandemic can be even more devastating than a world war. In 1918, the Great War, the war to end all wars,[1] ended. It had been an epic four-year battle that churned up Europe and ended with 25 million fewer people in the world. But as the war entered its final year the great influenza, the influenza to end all influenzas, put its plan of attack into motion.

The great influenza, or Spanish flu,[2] forged its way around the globe, conquering almost every country in the world. In total, the flu was victorious and claimed between 50 and 100 million lives: in half the time of the entire Great War it claimed over twice as many lives. No one is safe in pandemics, everyone is a target, and just like Spanish flu, the really evil pandemics don't discriminate[3]. If your immune system isn't up for a fight and can't defend itself, then this next war on your system could be the battle to end all of your battles: you're a living statistic waiting to be counted. And what's worse is that modern super drugs breed tougher super bugs. With every advance in medicine the virus mutates and finds chinks in our medical armour. So even with vaccines and hospitals on standby, when the next flu pandemic comes, a lot of us may be buggered.

WHEN WILL IT HAPPEN?	WHEN SHOULD I START TO PANIC?	WHAT WILL HAPPEN NEXT?
Soon, it *will* happen again. Steer clear of anyone, or anything, that you see sneezing.		Just like the First World War, the great influenza pandemic will spawn a sequel. A new outbreak will spread easily around the world through international travel.
WHAT SHOULD I LOOK FOR?		
A pet dies, then the owner dies, then the neighbour of the pet dies, then the neighbour's neighbour dies, etc ...	Coughs and sneezes spread diseases. Try not to add to the pandemonium.	With over four billion more people in the world since 1918 a new outbreak may spread even further ...

1. *See* World war three (166) • 2. It actually started in the USA: seems mean to blame the Spanish
3. SARS, Severe acute respiratory syndrome, is much more virulent than Spanish flu

IX

Look after number one

Look after number one. *luck··af·tear··num·burr··won* – one man's loss is another man's gain.

Although there's safety in numbers, when it comes to the human race you need to get yourself out of the starting blocks quickly. The survival of the fittest is becoming the survival of the fattest; it's dog eat dog out there. And that's the problem, eating dog, cow and lamb is all well and good[1] but the food is becoming sugarier, fattier, pumped with additives and stripped of goodness, and at the same time, man is getting lazy.

Resting on your laurels is fine in moderation, as long as you move around every now and again. It's time the human race started watching its weight and watching what it eats. The Earth's crushed laurels need to be kicked into shape as we're getting fatter, older and less fertile. Our bodies may soon give up on us as we've given up on our waistlines.

---

1. Except for the dog, although it depends which country you live in

IX

Ob

Obesity

(138)

Obesity. *oh·bee·city* – **when the world's waistline slips over the equator.**

Feeling the weight of the world on our shoulders is a common complaint, but for almost a quarter of the world's population they have the weight of the world on their shoulders, around their waist and on their ample bottom. The Industrial Revolution saw the human race progress faster than at any other time in its history, but it's also taken our busy buns out of the fields and placed our lazy asses firmly on chairs where they have stayed ever since. The size of our bellies impacts on more than our waistlines. It is estimated that by 2030 we will need 55% more food to feed these bigger bellies, especially as more people are becoming overweight or obese, and with an estimated two billion more mouths to feed by then, the fat are going to be taking up a much bigger slice of pie.

WHEN WILL IT HAPPEN?

We're already getting too big for our britches and we're only going to get bigger through bad diets and less movement.

Some estimates claim that over half the world is going to be overweight by 2030 but these figures may be inflated. When the fat lady sings, our health is going to suffer in a big way.

WHAT SHOULD I LOOK FOR?

Your toes.

WHEN SHOULD I START TO PANIC?

Obesity can be beaten but there's a fat chance that we'll collectively win the war on waistlines due to our bad diet and lack of exercise. Everyone in the developed world can get fat, including our kids, our pensioners and even our pets.

WEIGHT OF THE WORLD (%)

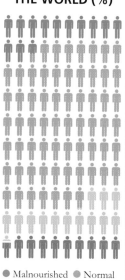

● Malnourished ● Normal
● Overweight ● Obese

Source: WHO/TUSPHTM

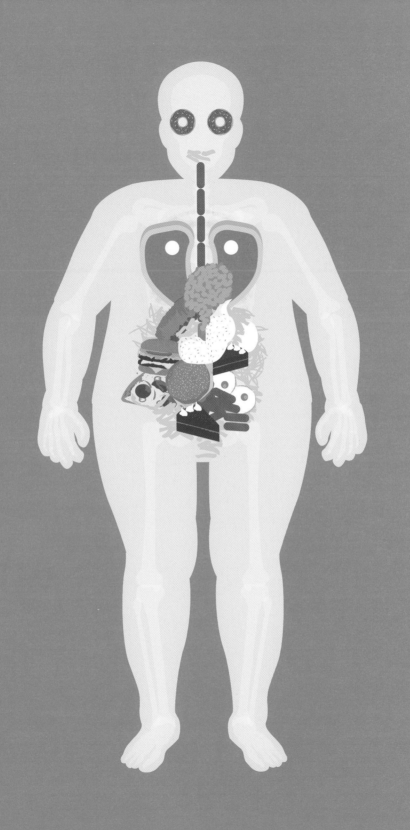

Mf

IX

Male infertility

(140)

Male infertility. *mayl··in·fur·till·it·ee* – 'mankind' could soon be renamed 'womankind'.

Man, the breadwinner of the human race, is totally expendable. There was a time when a world without man was physically impossible but through in vitro fertilisation, man has been made redundant; he has effectively become a name on a label on a test tube. And man isn't helping himself as, even though the world's population is rising, sperm counts are falling – a man's sperm can become as lazy as the couch potato they reside in.

When it comes to dropping your pants for the no-pants dance, offspring are not guaranteed, and an assault on a womb isn't going to be successful if your boys don't want to leave the barracks. Man could find himself on a shelf in a seed bank, in between the apes and the wheat, but man will never get replaced by a test tube: who would cut the grass?

WHAT SHOULD I LOOK FOR?

Large extruding bumps on female tummies that aren't linked to obesity.

WHAT SHOULD I DO NEXT?

The following list of conditions can cause low sperm counts: age, smoking, alcohol, tight pants, overheating, drug use, vitamin deficiency, certain types of food, obesity, varicose veins, toxic chemicals, heavy metals, genetic factors, stress, radiation and bicycling.

WHEN SHOULD I START TO PANIC?

The chances of giving birth to a boy are 50/50, so male heirs will be produced half of the time. Just over half of the world's population is male, so there really is one man for every woman, assuming a large proportion isn't gay.

WORLD POPULATION RATIO

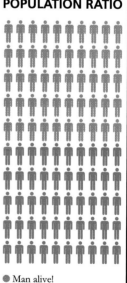

● Man alive!
● Woman's own

Source: CIA

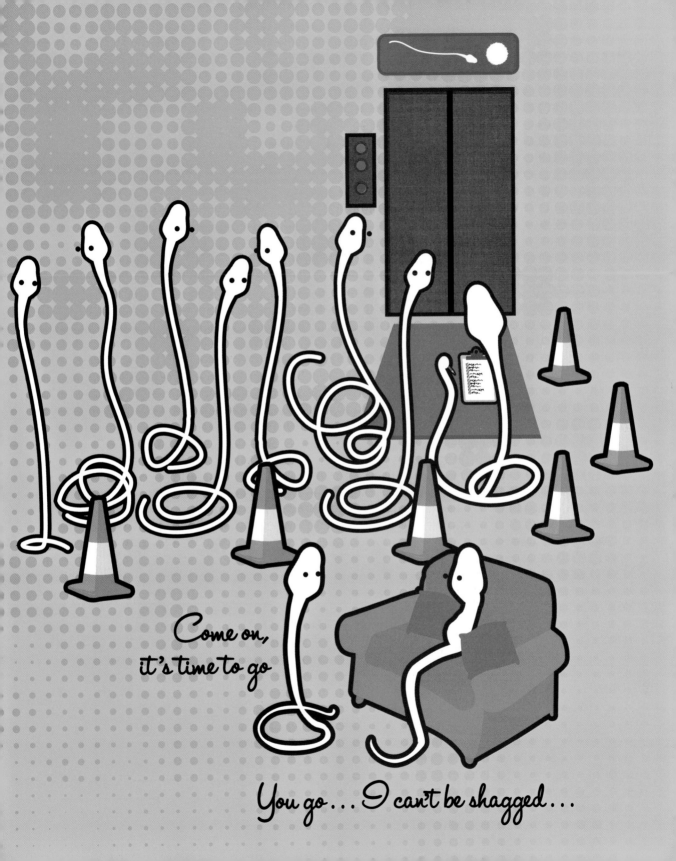

IX

Ae

Ageing
population

(142)

Ageing population. *a·jing··pop·you·lay·shon* – when old becomes the new young.

Dying is so last year. If you want to join the fastest growing gang in town then you'll need to meet at least two criteria: a) being alive and b) being over sixty years of age. Anything else is a bonus. The world's population is increasing and so is its collective age. Even a world war[1] only dents the population figures for a short time. In the UK, there are now more pensioners over sixty than youths under sixteen, which is typical of population trends in developed countries across the world. Medical discoveries and wonder potions are keeping us ticking over for longer, giving us more time to moan about our ailments. What's more, living conditions have improved since Victorian times, causing life expectancy to creep up. It used to be so rare to reach 100 that the Queen would send a telegram to the lucky centenarian but in modern times her royal duties have been sidelined because she spends most of her days signing telegrams for the many new members of the 100 club; and if she's anything like her mum, she'll be signing her own soon. With more pensioners cheating death, the system may not be able to cope, health services will be squeezed, pensions are under pressure and there is fuel poverty. It sounds like the best may not be yet to come.

WHAT SHOULD I LOOK FOR?

An increase in the sale of slippers and blankets at Christmas.

Longer queues than normal at the chemist and the post office.

Traffic moving even slower than normal on a Sunday afternoon.

More old people's homes than ordinary people's homes.

WHEN SHOULD I START TO PANIC?

You're always a second closer to being a pensioner yourself.

POSSIBILITY IT WILL HAPPEN?

Unless a massive catastrophe like a pandemic[2] strikes or a new freezing ice age that targets the old and the weak, we're stuck with them.

WHAT SHOULD I DO NEXT?

Turn your house into an old people's home, it'll bring in a bit of cash.

---

1. When millions of men were shipped off to get shot at; *see* World war three (166) • 2. *See* Pandemic (134)

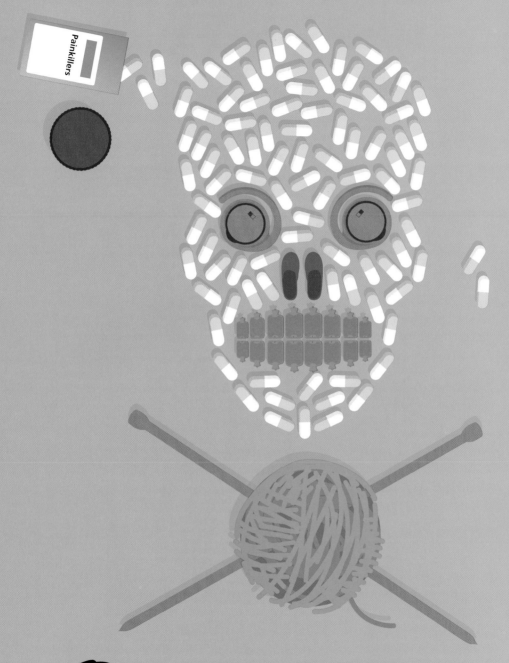

Old is the dead young ...

X
Predictions

Predictions. *pre·dick·shonz* – when the end is foretold in an interpreted and unconvincingly vague way.

The end of the world has been foretold countless times throughout Earth's history, and, so far, the human race is still here. Soothsayers, witches and sages have been replaced by scientists, environmentalists, satellites and early-warning systems, which predict our end in a similar way but with more evidence and accuracy. And although it's less eye of newt and wing of bat there is still a similar amount of scaremongery.

Witchcraft, telling of fortunes and predicting the future was once punishable by death, while modern-day predictions are made to estimate our possible and future punishing deaths, feeding the armchair scientists and sofasayers[1] with facts and fuel for extensive doommongery.

---

1. *See* Glossary (263)

X

Ma

Mayan
calendar: 2012

(146)

Mayan calendar. *my·ann··cal·end·are* – when the shortest day of the year becomes the last day of life on Earth.

Mayan society was an ancient civilisation that loved nothing better than solving maths problems. Their mathematical systems were made up of dots, lines and shells and even though they hadn't discovered numbers, their knowledge was so advanced that their calculations were more accurate than those of their European counterparts who had already discovered numbers. Along with sums and maths quizzes, the Mayans loved calendars, so much so that they cross-referenced the day by using three different types: a tall, a grande and a venti version.[1]

The 'venti' calendar was known as the long count. It was based on the tall and grande versions, which predicted only about fifty years into the future. By cross-referencing these two calendars the Mayans could create the long count, which predicted way into the future, centuries in fact. Upon the rediscovery of the Mayans' long count calendar, modern mathematicians number-crunched, decoded and transposed it on to our modern Gregorian calendar. It was discovered that the long count would end on 21 December 2012 ... precisely. For mathematicians it denotes the end of the current Mayan calendar cycle; for others it predicts the end of the world ...

WHEN WILL IT HAPPEN?

21 December 2012. Put this date in your diary. While you're updating your calendar of events, start opening your Advent calendar on 27 November, you can count down to the end of the world in 2012 instead of Christmas. Shame the only present could be death.

WHEN SHOULD I START TO PANIC?

Never trust soothsayers who don't know their own demise.

WHAT WILL HAPPEN NEXT?

Some predict the end, the second coming or a new age of man, while the majority predict last-minute Christmas shopping just like last year, and the next ...

WHAT SHOULD I DO NEXT?

In 2012, bring Christmas forward by a week.

1. Not to be confused with Mayan coffee cup sizes

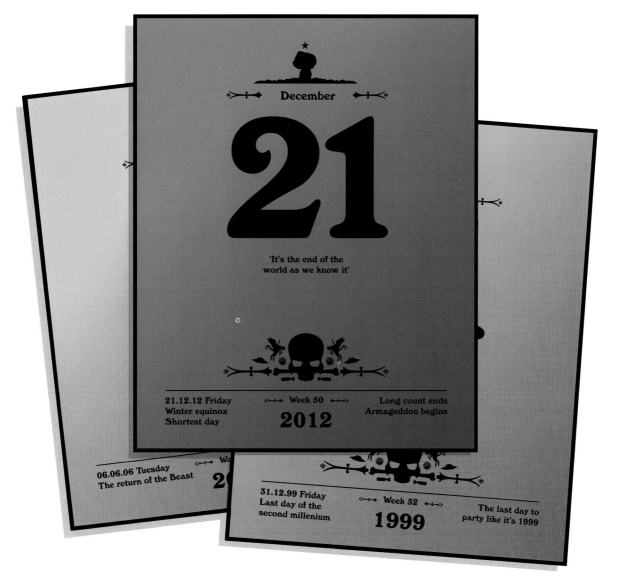

December

21

'It's the end of the
world as we know it'

21.12.12 Friday
Winter equinox
Shortest day

Week 50

2012

Long count ends
Armageddon begins

06.06.06 Tuesday
The return of the Beast

31.12.99 Friday
Last day of the
second millenium

Week 52

1999

The last day to
party like it's 1999

Modern-day Nostradami. *mod·urn··daye··noz·trow·darm·eye –* the original prophet of doom reloaded within us all.

Nostradamus, the original prophet of doom, was a sixteenth-century French astrologer who wrote thousands of prophecies predicting man's demise in thousands of different ways, including volcanic fires, the spilt blood of the just, not to mention plenty of death and destruction with a predominantly French tilt. In his day, Nostradamus couldn't have predicted the modern-day fascination with his bite-sized doommongery.[1] His prophecies have been twisted, contorted and bastardised into many freedictive[2] incarnations to cater for every major disaster: the Great Fire of London, the French Revolution, the rise of Hitler, the use of nuclear weapons, global warming and the terror attacks on the Twin Towers, amongst many others. But if his predictions are so well respected then why have none of them ever been used to prevent such disasters? It's because they're open to interpretation, giving no solid dates or names, which leads to misinterpretation. But at heart we're all modern-day Nostradami, everyone has a view on climate change, melting glaciers and extinction rates, with equally dubious percentages to match. As Einstein once said, 'If the facts don't fit the theory, change the facts.' He's got a point, say it like you mean it and for the average sofasayer,[2] fiction becomes fact.

WHEN WILL IT HAPPEN?

When murderous chaos touches the land, a wave of great turmoil will commence. **Translation:** Be prepared, as something could vaguely happen at any unspecified time.

WHAT SHOULD I LOOK FOR?

Bad things that fit into a Nostradamus vision.

WHEN SHOULD I START TO PANIC?

Not just yet but we predict you should panic sometime in the future.

HOW TO BECOME A SOOTHSAYER

Write thousands of predictions. The more you write, the more chance you have of a prediction coming true.

Omit names of places or people.

Adding names will limit the scope for interpretation.

Say it like you mean it and it becomes fact.

---

1. If he was a halfway decent soothsayer he would've • 2. *See* Glossary (263)

XI

Little issues

Little issues. *lit·tall··ish·shoes* – size isn't important in this small world; it's not what you've got, it's what you do with it that counts.

By delving into the world of the very tiny, we created a very big and uncomfortable situation for ourselves. By fiddling around with the minute building blocks of life we've created a world where the power of atoms can be released with the push of a button that will send us all to oblivion, including you and your nuclear family. Once upon a time our world was easy to understand, as everything could be explained by _____.[1]

It was believed that anything smaller than a speck of dust was impossible, after all, the Bible claims that God made Adam from dust, and Adam made you and I; but the advent of microscopes has shown that dust is made up of even smaller elements ... Ashes to ashes, dust to dust, atoms to atoms, sub-atomic particles to sub-atomic particles, neutrons to neutrons, quarks to quarks ... The world of the small has become a very big issue.

---

1. Please insert your deity or deities here

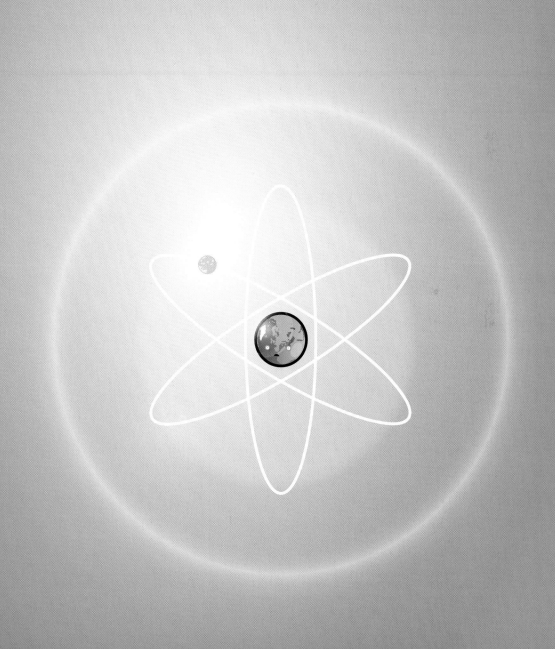

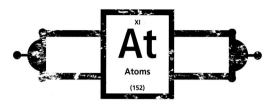

XI

At

Atoms

(152)

Atoms. *at·ums* – impossible to see with the naked eye, but can still be coaxed to perform the splits.

Sometime in the BC, a group of Greek[1] philosophers took the afternoon off from a hard day's thought to celebrate a fellow philosopher's birthday. As the hungry philosophers waited for the birthday boy[2] to arrive they began to eat the food. When he finally turned up, the last of his cake had gone. Democritus, who was the only one who had waited for him to show up before eating his piece of cake, split his slice into two equal parts and gave one half to the birthday latecomer.

At this moment Democritus hypothesised that if he keep dividing his cake, he would eventually reach an indivisible plateau where he could no longer divide his cake. He announced his idea to his peers as *atomon* (uncuttable), and particle physics was born. He then promptly stuffed his face with the atom-rich birthday dessert.

It took thousands of years for his theory to be proved right, but it wasn't just birthday cake that was made up of indivisible atoms, everything around us is, including ourselves. It seemed nothing could be smaller. But then, like an atomic pass-the-particle, the atom was unwrapped, making the indivisible, divisible. Each layer was peeled away, uncovering sub-atomic particle parcels. All the scientists' birthdays came at once, leaving the rest of us in fear that we may have witnessed our last.

WHEN WILL IT HAPPEN?

It already has. Splitting the atom opened the door for nuclear war.

WHAT SHOULD I LOOK FOR?

A cloud that resembles a mushroom on the horizon, and hot winds.

WHEN SHOULD I START TO PANIC?

WHAT SHOULD I DO NEXT?

Prepare for a Nuclear Winter, Spring, Summer and Autumn.

ALL THE SMALL THINGS

It is believed that a speck of dust contains around 3 trillion atoms.

1. Also known as 'Geek' philosophers by the detractors of the time • 2. The name of the birthday boy has been forgotten; history doesn't remember the latecomers

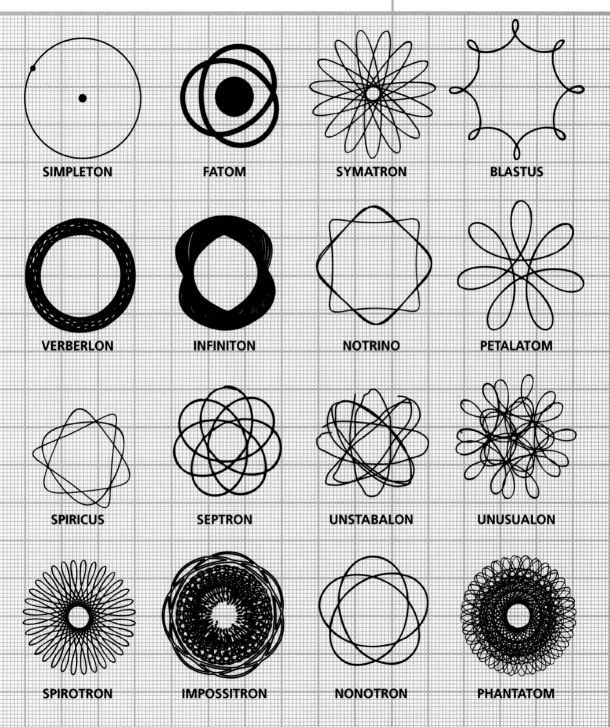

SOME ATOMS OF NOTE

SERIES 7

SIMPLETON

FATOM

SYMATRON

BLASTUS

VERBERLON

INFINITON

NOTRINO

PETALATOM

SPIRICUS

SEPTRON

UNSTABALON

UNUSUALON

SPIROTRON

IMPOSSITRON

NONOTRON

PHANTATOM

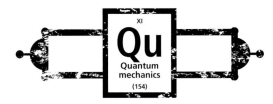

Qu
XI
Quantum mechanics
(154)

Quantum mechanics. *kwan·tum··meck·ann·niks* – the study of the very *very* small, even smaller than the smallest possible thing.

The world was once neat and orderly. What went up came back down again. Everything behaved itself, the maths had proved it. Then an extreme form of maths gained popularity, causing the world, in theory, to descend into chaos. Atoms, the smallest things that were thought to exist, turned out to be massive compared to the protons, neutrons and electrons, quarks and gluons that were discovered hiding inside.

Muon

Muon-neutrino

Electron

Electron-neutrino

The quantum mechanics observed the particles in their natural habitat and found their world to be chaotic and lawless. The laws that existed in our land of the giants refused to be adhered to in the sub-atomic world. Nothing made sense any more and all sorts of new particles and anti-particles were thrown into the mix. Chaos reigned and what used to go up didn't always come back down again, and if it did, it sometimes came down in two different places at the same time. Nuclear physicists took to physically abusing their share of sub-atomic particles: they ripped them apart, generally crashed them together and relatively beat them up.

To make the best possible sense of it all, the long-understood forces were

WHAT SHOULD I LOOK FOR?

Atoms are too small to be seen with the naked eye as they're really teeny weeny. But keep an eye out for an ever expanding black hole appearing on the Swiss–French border that may engulf the Earth.

WHEN SHOULD I START TO PANIC?

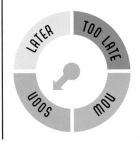

LATER · TOO LATE · NOW · SOON

QUANTUMS OF SOLACE

Atoms have protons
and anti-particles,
Hadron colliders
with steady
stream trickles,
Bosons and Leptons
all tied up with strings,
This is a list of
some atomic things.

---

1. Forces at work: strong, weak, electromagnetic and gravitational force • 2. *See* Multiverse (236)
3. The Higgs boson is the missing link of the atomic world. This currently hypothetical particle would

forced together[1] in the hope that they'd unite in a new equation that would help us understand our crazy cosmos, but, as scientists discovered, you can fling the forces together but you can't make them unify.

Tau

Tau-neutrino

Scientists had to think outside the box. Once traditional thinking was pushed aside, scientist discovered that the box was tied up with a unifying thread, and string theory was born. This theory predicts that sub-atomic particles are actually made up of infinitesimal strings that vibrate in varied ways, giving the particles different signatures. But when they reopened the box that had been tied up in string theory, they got more than they bargained for: the box was not only full of string, but it also contained, multiverses[2] and anti-particles and other hypothetical particles such as the Higgs boson.[3] It seemed that this theory came with even more strings attached than were anticipated, even though the theory is completely tamper proof.[4] As for the newly discovered particles, the only way to test their validity and prove their existence was to build a very big and expensive experiment.

Charm

Strange

The Large Hadron Collider, a particle accelerator, was built by CERN,[5] with the purpose of sending particles racing around a massive circuit in opposite directions where they're pushed to 99.99% of the speed of light, which were then sacrificed into each other to spill their chaotic innards for scientists to dissect the quantum amount of their remains. By creating such a powerful machine, it was also supposed that theoretical particles called stranglets could be created that may destroy the Earth via an uncontrollable chain reaction triggered by the experiment, which would also trigger the end of the world via a mini black hole.

Up quark

Down quark

Top quark

Bottom quark

These claims were dismissed and on 10 September 2008, when the first successful experiment was conducted and no Earth-eating black holes were produced, it was thought that the holes in the theory were exposed. But just nine days later the collider catastrophically failed, proving that the unforeseen cannot be accounted for, so maybe there is still cause for conCERN after all?

---

solve the issue of the missing mass within atoms • 4. The theory of vibrating strings is rock solid as it can neither be proved nor disproved because a microscope powerful enough to see them can never be invented • 5. The European organisation for nuclear research.

XI

Na

Nano-
technology

(156)

Nanotechnology. *nan·no·tek·noll·lodge·ee* – Nano, nano: it's off to work we go; the science of very small robots.

Nanotechnology is the science of manipulating matter at an atomic level to suit a particular need. Nanotechnology begins with the creation of carbon nanotubes, which become the building blocks of nanostructures. Carbon is incredibly versatile: all living things contain carbon, you can also burn it as coal or wear it in diamonds. The application for the nanotubes seems limitless: they can be used in everything from electronic circuits to medicine. They could create strong fibres and clothes, making light materials stronger than steel. This technology has already been deployed in various products, ranging from computers to cosmetics, and it is hoped that nanotechnology will benefit us all medically, but nanophobia is beginning to creep in, especially when it comes to nanoparticles coming into contact with the skin. There is a fear that the nanoparticles might squeeze through the skin and travel around the body on a mini rampage, irreparably damaging organs as they go. So the technology that's been created to remove the need for long stints in hospital may possibly begin to destroy us from the inside out, forcing us to spend our final days staring at the inside of a hospital we were never supposed to see again. It's enough to make you sick to death of technology.

WHEN WILL IT HAPPEN?	WHEN SHOULD I START TO PANIC?	WHAT SHOULD I DO NEXT?
Nanotechnology has already been deployed in electronic circuits, computer hardware, cosmetics, kitchenware, automobiles, clothing, sporting goods, paint, personal-care items, home furnishings, food and drink, automotive and medical products, to name but a few.	 Nanotechnology hasn't been proven to be harmful ... yet.	You could try to avoid products with nano-particles in, but there are no legal requirements for companies to list nanotechnology on the packaging, plus you're exposed to nanotech-nology daily. Just keep an eye on your DNA: if it starts breaking down, consult your doctor.

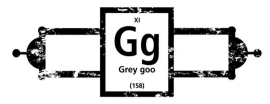

Grey goo. *grae··goo* – **when self-replicating atomic machines born from nanotechnology don't know the meaning of the word 'stop'.**

Building on a small scale is hard. Either you'll need a very steady hand and eyes that can zoom to be able to see individual atoms or you'll need to create a very small workforce to build the items, one atom at a time. This is where nanobots come in.

Our tiny friends could do all our tiny dirty work for us. These little slaves could build our world using carbon nanostructures from the atom up. They could create hard-wearing clothing, strengthen our buildings, help repair our broken bones or they may pick on something their own size by starting fights with the viruses that cause our winter colds. As nanotechnology advances, more complex and elaborate machines will be created and it's been predicted that a nanobot could build everything from appliances to food. It's also been predicted that if these robots mutate and self-replicate then they might not know when to stop. In a worst-case scenario, the robots would self-replicate to such an extent that the billions of robots swarming together trying to fulfil their mission would create a kind of grey goo that would engulf everything in its path whilst at the same time returning the organic material it encountered back to its basic atomic matter. As it replicated further it would eventually engulf the entire Earth. So if your nanobots don't turn up for work one day then God help us all – once they start running amok, they'll run us into the ground.

WHEN WILL IT HAPPEN?	**WHEN SHOULD I START TO PANIC?**	**WHAT SHOULD I LOOK FOR?**
It won't happen just yet as the technology is still being developed, but wait fifty years or so and if you encounter a mass of grey heading towards you, get off the planet as quick as you can.		The planet falling apart around you. Excruciating pain as the bots turn you back into atoms. **GET WITH THE PROGRAM** **1** Self-replicate, **2** Go to **1**, **3** Run

XI

Am

Ancient
microbes

(160)

Ancient microbes. *aint·chant··my·krobes* – ancient diseases from the past that are about to get medieval on your future ass.

The polar regions of the Earth are nature's refrigerators: everything that is covered over with fresh layers of snow is perfectly preserved under its icy blanket. Year after year, new coverings of snow are laid on top of each other, eventually compacting and turning into ice. This ice traps whatever happens to have been blown, has landed or died there: whether it be plant pollen, seagull or woolly mammoth, they'll be completely frozen in time. As well as its refrigerated hors d'œuvres and meat selections, the ice also contains mini air bubbles that contain tiny samples of the air from when the snow was laid, giving a unique record of the climate at that time. Over the years the layers get thicker and thicker and in certain parts of Antarctica they can record the last 80,000 years, creating a climate record for scientific time travellers. To retrieve the data, ice samples are drilled and the core is extracted, creating a cylindrical ice cube many metres long. But there may also be hidden microbes from the past stored inside the ice, waiting for a little bit of warmth to defrost, creating the ideal moment to infect their victims. If the core starts to thaw then we really could be skating on thin ice.

WHEN WILL IT HAPPEN?	WHEN SHOULD I START TO PANIC?	WHAT WILL HAPPEN NEXT?
The ice caps and permafrost are defrosting. As long as the scientists shut the freezer door after getting the milk out, the ice cores should stay frozen. Keep an eye out for personality changes or unusual behaviour in your colleagues. You may have to put them out of their misery.	 When you can hear only silence from the other end of the Antarctic radio.	If killer microbes are released through ice core drilling the victims should be contained in the remote parts, such as Antarctica, Siberia or the Arctic. This could prevent millions of deaths around the world, as long as the victims don't take leave to warmer climates.

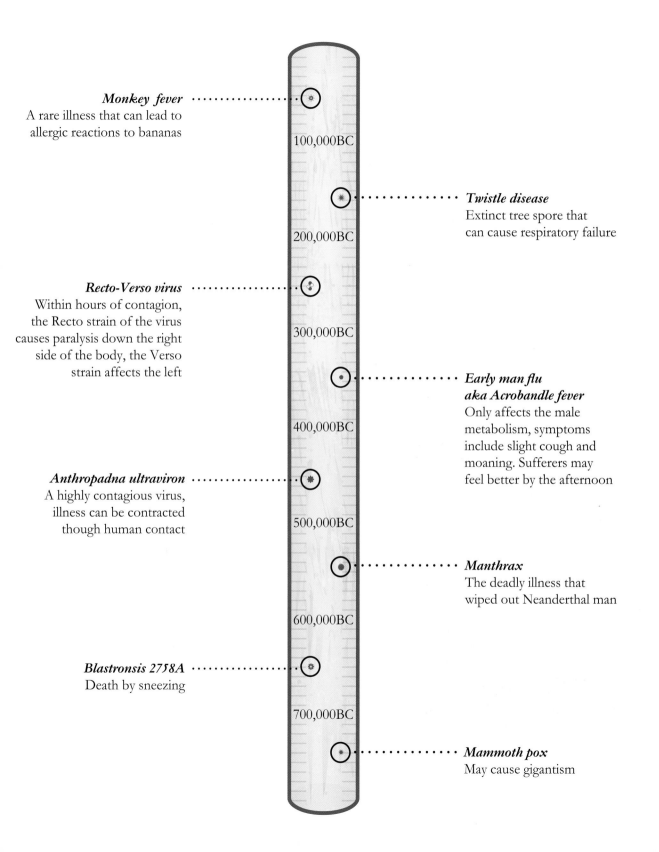

Monkey fever
A rare illness that can lead to
allergic reactions to bananas

100,000BC

Twistle disease
Extinct tree spore that
can cause respiratory failure

200,000BC

Recto-Verso virus
Within hours of contagion,
the Recto strain of the virus
causes paralysis down the right
side of the body, the Verso
strain affects the left

300,000BC

**Early man flu
aka Acrobandle fever**
Only affects the male
metabolism, symptoms
include slight cough and
moaning. Sufferers may
feel better by the afternoon

400,000BC

Anthropadna ultraviron
A highly contagious virus,
illness can be contracted
though human contact

500,000BC

Manthrax
The deadly illness that
wiped out Neanderthal man

600,000BC

Blastronsis 2758A
Death by sneezing

700,000BC

Mammoth pox
May cause gigantism

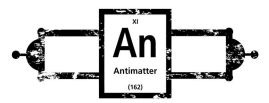

Antimatter. *auntie··mat·tear* – when particles and anti-particles meet, it's no laughing matter.[1]

Matter is all around you, from the Earth to the stars; everything in the visible universe is made up of matter. But matter has an invisible evil twin, a twin that's so destructive, it's locked away out of sight, out of mind. If antimatter is tempted out of its hideout, then when matter and antimatter meet, it'll end in murder.

Anti-particles are exactly the same as particles in every way but with an opposite electrical charge. When anti-particles come into contact with particles then they're both completely annihilated, so this must mean that matter, which is made up of particles, must also have an anti-twin.[2]

The known Universe is leftover matter from the big bang. In the beginning there was an unequal balance of matter and antimatter; both elements annihilated each other and what was left is the matter you see around you – and this creation and anticreation still goes on, every single day. Gamma rays are the product of daily annihilation.

But there is a theory that way out there in space there may be galaxies that are made entirely of antimatter, the antigalaxies to our galaxies, and if they come into contact it may be a matter of life and death for us here on Earth.

WHEN WILL IT HAPPEN?

Unknown but if our galaxy and an antigalaxy come into contact we'll be instantly vaporised.

WHAT SHOULD I LOOK FOR?

A massive antigalaxy hoving into view.

You may experience conflicting feelings just before you perish.

WHEN SHOULD I START TO PANIC?

As we have no idea if antigalaxies exist, it doesn't really matter.

WHAT SHOULD I DO NEXT?

All you can do is wait and see but in the meantime you can ponder the big questions, such as what caused the big bang?

Did an antigalaxy collide with a normal galaxy? And does this mean that there is an antiverse for our Universe?

---

1. Or the flipside is no laughing antimatter • 2. *See* Quantum mechanics (154)

XII

They'll kill us all

They'll kill us all. *they·ll··kill··uz··all* – when your whole life is dictated by a handful of individuals who play with fire while they play havoc with your emotions. It's not all fun and games.

You'd like to think that your life is in your own hands but unfortunately it isn't, a sleight-of-hand magic trick has been performed on you to make you think it is. We're all at the mercy of many individuals who make our decisions for us with wonderful/disastrous/unhelpful/hilarious[1] consequences.

Our world leaders take our countries' affairs down dangerous paths,[2] the banks punish us for their mistakes when it's their faults not ours,[3] rogue individuals perform hit-and-runs on our wallets,[4] whilst others are just in it to terrorise us.[5] So when everyone is out to get you, playing follow the leader isn't always the best option, playing dodge ball may be a better choice, at least you know what comes next ...

1. Delete where applicable to you • 2. *See* World war three (166) • 3. *See* Economic Collapse (178) 4. *See* Rogues (180) • 5 *See* Terrorism (184)

XII

Wiii

**World war
three**

(166)

World war three. *wurld··war··three* – the third and final part in
the trilogy.

Until 100 years ago, wars were localised protests fought between two
nations but the twentieth century saw wars beefed up into global contests.
The Great War – WWI (1914–1918), the first war in the trilogy, got totally
out of hand. It started with the usual local incident in a small corner of the
world, but within months had escalated into a worldwide ruckus. Everyone
was declaring war on everyone else and a war that started with the death
of one person[1] ended four years later with the deaths of over 15 million
more.[2] Described as the 'War to End All Wars' ... it wasn't. It ended with
victory for the good guys and defeat for the bad. It remained the bloodiest
war for over twenty years until the sequel to end all sequels was released.

When the empire struck back in 1939, the second part, *World War II
(1939–1945)*, turned out to be even bloodier than the original. The death
toll, budget and special effects were huge and this time the bad guys were
even worse. Germany was seeking revenge for the first war, and the second
one rumbled on for five turbulent years, with a death toll in excess of 55
million. Eventually the bad guys were defeated yet again. A war that was
started by a maniacal mad man[3] was ended by a mechanical little boy and

WHEN WILL IT HAPPEN?

World war three has
threatened ever since
the end of world war
two. It hangs over us
like fall-out from a
mushroom cloud.

WHAT SHOULD I LOOK FOR?

Whatever's left in the
world, salvage what you
can.

WHEN SHOULD I START TO PANIC?

Missiles already point in
your direction, get ready
to make a quick exocet.

NUCLEAR FAMILY

China, France, India,
Israel, Pakistan, Russia,
the United Kingdom
and the United States
have the bomb. Iran,
North Korea and Syria
are pursuing it. South
Africa used to have it
and Belgium, Germany,
Italy, the Netherlands,
Turkey and Greece
share it.

---

1. Franz Ferdinand • 2. Soldiers and civilians • 3. Hitler • 4. The names of the bombs dropped on
Hiroshima and Nagasaki

a fat man.[4] Unlike the first part, the second act ended on a cliff-hanger. Even though the bad guys were defeated, in the closing moments of the Second World War, there was a glimpse towards the third and final act of the trilogy coming soon to a country near you, *World War III – The Photon Menace.*

A nuclear war to end all wars, and all lives, has been in production ever since the end of part two, but so far, even though it's been fully financed, after a number of false starts, part three has never gone into full production. When it's finally released on the world, expect an initial and immediate big impact with counter-reactions from the rest of the world.

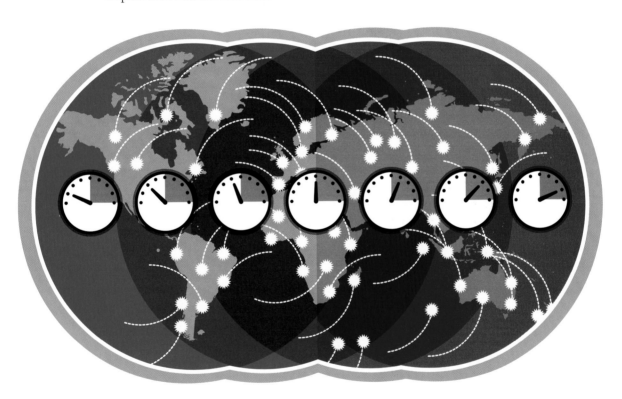

The impact of the third part in this long awaited trilogy will be brief but massively huge and everyone will be affected by it. And although the date has been altered throughout the last few decades, it's guaranteed that the takings will be enormous.

Nuclear weapons. *new·clear·wep·onz* – arms that cause harm

The threat of nuclear war has been hanging over us ever since the teaser ending of the Second World War, when two nuclear bombs were exploded in Japan, taking around 110,000 people with them instantly and leaving the rest of us in nuclear fear. Since 1945, no other nuclear bombs have been dropped in anger but plenty have been pointed in your face with intent. With a push of the red button, a chain of events will be put into motion that will take human existence to the precipice of extinction, if not right over the edge into oblivion. Nuclear bombs were built to inflict a maximum amount of damage with the minimum amount of effort and once they were released and unleashed on the world, everyone wanted them. A race to stockpile more weapons than your enemy began, creating a new cold war from a very hot one. The cold war was a tense stand-off between the two superpowers that emerged on top from the Second World War: the USA and the Soviet Union. Other countries joined in the nuclear muscle-flexing, resulting in a 'my warhead's bigger than yours' competition. But the irony is that if a nuclear strike is launched by one country on another then the targeted country will retaliate against its aggressor, causing equal and devastating destruction. It's a global game of nuclear chicken with all human life in the balance – luckily no one has pressed the button ... yet.

WHEN WILL IT HAPPEN?	WHEN SHOULD I START TO PANIC?	DON'T MENTION THE NUCLEAR WAR
The threat of nuclear war is always hanging over us. Tension between nuclear prolific countries doesn't help the situation either.		Nuclear war came close through the Cuban missile crisis in 1962. And in 1983, the USSR's nuclear early-warning system mistook clouds for a nuclear attack.[1] In the same year, the Soviets confused a NATO exercise for the precursor to a nuclear attack.[2]
WHAT SHOULD I LOOK FOR? The Nuclear Non-Proliferation Treaty signed by every single nation.	When you see fungus-shaped clouds, fall into the fall-out procedure.	

1. We owe our existence to Stanislav Petrov, a Russian lieutenant colonel who saved our bacon from an accidental nuclear war by overriding the Soviet nuclear launch computer that claimed that the clouds were actually a nuclear missile attack from the USA • 2. The Soviets thought that the Europe-wide NATO exercise, code-named Able Archer, was real preparation for a nuclear strike

XII

WI

World leaders

(170)

World leaders. *wurld··lee·derz* – when you should pick on someone your own size.

The world is like one enormous playground where dangerous games like hide-and-seek,[1] Chinese whispers, conquerors[2] and war games are played out on a massive scale. In this yard, friendships are forged and broken, the bigger bullies gang up on the smaller nations and a little pushing and shoving can lead to fights breaking out that can expand across the entire schoolyard; but when the bell goes these disagreements can be discussed and talked over in the classroom. This classroom is known as the United Nations. The UN consists of the 192 countries of the world.[3] It's a place where each country can express its unique opinion on the way affairs are being conducted in the unruly playground, and like most classes the students don't always see eye to eye. The UN consists of uncontrollable students and uncompromising views. Countries can be unpredictable and untrustworthy, unsympathetic, unreasonable and unneighbourly; unpopular, ungrateful and downright uncooperative. Unfortunately, this global therapy session can only go so far and when the home-time bell rings the problems of the world spill back out into the unregulated playground, where new war games are waiting to be played and fought out.

WHEN WILL IT HAPPEN?

Nations are constantly falling out with each other. The world is full of bullying and intolerance, wars are kicking off all the time. Let's hope it's not a nuclear one.

WHAT SHOULD I LOOK FOR?

Escalating tyranny.

WHEN SHOULD I START TO PANIC?

When your leader's words have more to do with warfare than welfare.

OTHER UN-RELATED WORDS

unloved, unstatesman-like, unparliamentary, untroubled, unofficial, unsuccessful, unkindly, unsupported, unleash-ed, unjust, unprepared, unsurprised, untruthful, unspecified, unwav-ering, unprofessional, unorthodox, unstopp-able, unpronounceable, unsociable.

---

1. The USA and its allies played hide-and-seek with Weapons of Mass Destruction in Iraq. The weapons were hidden so well that none were ever found • 2. Or 'Conkers' for short • 3. Kosovo, Taiwan and the Vatican City do not belong to the UN. Taiwan is not yet recognised as a separate country from China

XII

Gh

Global hegemony

(172)

Global hegemony. *glow·bull·· hedg·ee·money* – **when my country is bigger than yours.**

The game of global one-upmanship is a very dangerous one to play, as the bigger they are the harder they fall, which, in these days of globalisation, has worldwide consequences. Over the centuries, countries have played pass-the-superpower-parcel and leapfrogged each other to become the world's primary dominant leader. A dominant global empire can reign for centuries but just like the Romans, the British, the Spanish and the Superpower of the Soviet Union, they either become a pale shadow of their former selves or end up resigned to Empirical history, even though, for a time, it looks like they can never be superseded. Since the end of the Second World War, the world has been dominated by the USA, but of late, even the mighty USA has become weak at the knees due to economic pressures, bankruptcy and rogues, resulting in a worldwide credit crisis. The beginning of the end for the US may have already begun with the actions of the exceedingly greedy and some total and utter bankers.[1] For every superpower that loses its super ability there's always another country waiting to exert influence on the rest of the world. Next in line for super status are the developing nations of China and India, waiting to go head to head in an all new superpower showdown.

WHEN WILL IT HAPPEN?	**WHEN SHOULD I START TO PANIC?**	**POWER CUTS**
It's a long way to fall when your superpowers begin to fail you. The loss of your powers could be a temporary glitch as they may be regained, but it'll take a lot of time, money and the fall of a larger power than yours for you to become powerful once again.	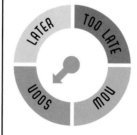 If the big guns fall then be prepared for world-wide fall-out.	Previous reigns include: The Roman Empire, the Byzantine Empire, the Arab Empire, the Bulgarian Empire, the Frankish Empire, the Holy Roman Empire, the Tang Dynasty, the Mongol Empire, the Venetian Republic, the British Empire, the Ottoman Empire and the Russian Empire.

1. *See* Economic collapse (178) and Rogues (180)

XII
Glo
Globalisation
(174)

Globalisation. *glow·bull·eyz·a·chon* – when countries become bed-fellows and reap produce.

Jumping into bed with a strange country and getting straight down to business is all part of modern trading. If handled well then this consenting monetary transaction can reap financial rewards.

By forging polygamous relationships, every partner benefits from the skills that the other partaking countries provide. Globalisation means countries are jumping in and out of each other's beds faster than you can say 'in arrears', and this will continue as long as your country keeps its attractive assets. Promiscuity is rife on the open market and countries will tout their trade to anyone, hoping someone will make them an offer they can't refuse. But globalisation isn't all fun and games.

When a country's growth is affected, the resulting downturn can affect a country's performance, which, in an open market, can also infect the performance of other countries. The affliction can then spread, which in turn becomes an epidemic. What used to go up just stays down.

This can all be avoided by taking the right precautions – otherwise you'll end up feeling used and abused, battered and bruised, and left with a very empty wallet and a globally infectious situation.

WHEN WILL IT HAPPEN?	WHEN SHOULD I START TO PANIC?	WHAT SHOULD I DO NEXT?
Globalisation is happening all around you. Your pants are made in China, your socks are Indian. The money to pay for all this is in a Swiss bank account. Your kids' toys are made in Taiwan. Your kitchen is Swedish, the plumber is from Poland and your wife is from Thailand.	 The USA has been infected and we're catching the disease.	The rainy day you've been saving for has come in the form of a torrential downpour. The failed US property market has plunged the entire world into deep water and the flood waters keep rising. It's time to dip into your rainy-day funds to buy a lifeboat.

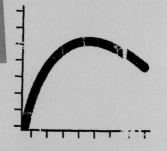

XII

Bk

Bankruptcy

(176)

Bankruptcy. *bank·rup·see* – when X owes Y but hasn't got the Gs to pay the I.O.U.

Banking used to be simple: you put your money in the bank for safe keeping and removed it when you needed it. But when the banks get greedy and try to turn your slow hard-earned pennies into fast easy bucks, then you may as well have taken your money out of the hole in the wall and flushed it down the drain, as you may never see it again. Trust in the banking sector is everything, and when it fails, it fails spectacularly.

The global credit crunch, which began in 2007, saw long-established companies collapse in bankruptcy. Not only that, financial institutions that were once thought untouchable, erupted, taking billions of pounds with them in the resulting fireball. Everyone and everything has been affected, from Freddies, Fannies and Adams to Brothers, Bears, Wool and even Rocks.[1] Entire countries have come close to collapse.[2] The lucky ones are bailed out or bought up, the unlucky ones are filed away in the dustbin of business history.

But the ultimate irony is that a government bail-out of a financial institution is only possible through the cash that you've paid in taxes, so in a strange turn of events you end up owning part of the bank you used to bank with. But will you reap any of the benefits? You can't bank on it.

WHEN WILL IT HAPPEN?	WHEN SHOULD I START TO PANIC?	WHAT SHOULD I DO NEXT?
Bankruptcy is a common occurrence in business but during the current credit crunch, it seems no one is safe from credit crunching.		Don't put all your eggs in one basket. Spread your money around, as if the bank breaks, so will most of your eggs, if not all of them. The current credit crunch has already turned many banks' assets into a credit brunch, breaking our eggs whilst trying to save their bacon.
WHAT SHOULD I LOOK FOR?		
Unchecked lottery tickets or coins down the side of the sofa.	When tax payers' cash bails out the IMF piggy bank too[3] ...	

---

1. Freddie Mac & Fannie Mae (US Mortgage providers), Adams (UK Clothing outlet), Lehman Brothers (US investment bank), Bear Stearns (US investment bank), Woolworths (UK high street store), Northern Rock (UK building society) • 2. Iceland (a European country) amongst others • 3. *See* Economic collapse (178)

Stuff4Sale

When you can get the best for less

| Bankruptcy sales | Countries and currencies ⇕ | **GO** |

*** GENUINE Iceland ***

A once in a lifetime chance to own the stunning country of Iceland – the land of fire and ...

$9.99   0 Bids   1m 52s

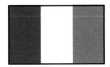

France

This is your opportunity to own one of the world's most famous European countries ...

$14.02   14 Bids   7m 44s

United States Must Go!

Your chance to own one of the greatest and youngest countries in the world. Starting at ...

$18.71   2 Bids   23m 13s

Bank of England *Cheap*

Get pounds for pence with this lot. The Bank of England is on sale for as little as ...

$42.50   11 Bids   31m 01s

The UK can be yours

The land of Shakespeare is up for grabs. The UK could be yours for ...

$27.45   21 Bids   45m 59s

Real Sale – Hungary!

Your chance to own a piece of the European community at a bargain starting price of ...

$32.75   7 Bids   58m 17s

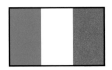

Viva Italia _ Bargain **

This ancient civilisation can be yours. Bid high for a chance to own the home of the Romans ...

$31.54   24 Bids   59m 48s

Euro vision

The currency that has out performed the dollar and the pound is now up for sale ...

$9.99   0 Bids   1m 52s

LOOK!!! Bank of America

A licence to print your own money with the currency that was once ...

$9.99   0 Bids   1m 52s

XII

Ec

Economic
collapse

(178)

Economic collapse. *eee·kon·omik··col·lapse* – when the economy of an entire country plunges into economic gloom and the cash in your pocket becomes worth less, then worthless.

Global economies are as stable as the elastic on an old pair of pants. During the good times the pants stayed up for years but over time the rot has set in and eventually, after ignoring the signs, the pants start to fall, causing them to hit rock bottom. But unlike the pants, you can't fix the economy with a new bit of elastic, hoping that it'll bounce back.

The way to prevent a collapse is to heed the warnings from history and do something about them. In 1923, Germany went through a period of hyperinflation, resulting in a time when it was cheaper to heat the house by burning money than buying wood, and the Wall Street Crash of 1929 plunged America into a great depression, causing a global downturn and years of hardship before anyone could restart the cash well.[1] Unfortunately, it's happened again. The problems that began with the US housing market have affected the majority of the world's economies, and in another 2008 economic disaster, Zimbabwe's bank notes had more zeros than 'Zimbabwean dollar' written in binary code.[2] But this time, the world has a secret stack of cash hidden under the mattress.

WHEN WILL IT HAPPEN?	WHEN SHOULD I START TO PANIC?	TRACKS ON THE IMF's STEREO
When it takes billions of pounds to buy a single penny sweet.		Dire Straits: 'Money For Nothing', The Beatles: 'Help!', A Tribe Called Quest: 'I Left My Wallet in El Segundo', ABBA: 'Money, Money, Money', Elvis: 'In The Ghetto', 50 Cent: 'Piggy Bank', The Fall: 'F-'oldin' Money', Patti Smith: 'Free Money', Johnny Cash: 'Cry! Cry! Cry!'
WHAT SHOULD I LOOK FOR?		
When the phrase 'I promise to pay the bearer' no longer bears any meaning. Long queues at the bank due to cashless cash machines.	When your rainy-day savings have been washed away by bank-eruptcy.	

---

1. 'Restart the cash well' is an anagram of 'the Wall Street Crash' • 2. That's 64 zeros in binary code
3. With the exception of seven UN members: North Korea, Cuba, Andorra, Monaco, Liechtenstein, Tuvalu, and Nauru and the three non-UN members: Kosovo, Taiwan and the Vatican City

The International Monetary Fund, or IMF, and the World Bank were established after the great depression and in the wake of the Second World War in 1945, to help stabilise the world's finances and prevent this kind of situation happening again. The IMF consists of 185 of 195 countries of the world[3] who stockpile their cash together to create a giant joint account that can be accessed only when a country gets into financial difficulty; it's like a worldwide cash machine that is accessible when all a country has left in its pockets are I.O.U.s.

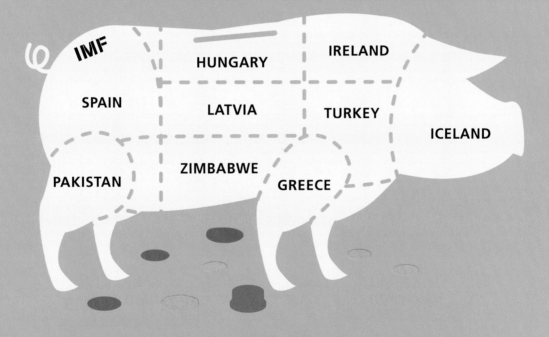

But the booms and the busts continue, and in 2007 the world was hit with a global credit crunch that turned into a crisis. Country after country queued up at the IMF's cashpoint, including Iceland, Turkey, Latvia and Pakistan, each withdrawing billions of pounds. But as the crisis deepens the queue will get longer, the debt will grow deeper and the money will run dry. So when it comes to the crunch, it looks like the world's economies have bitten off more than we can collectively chew.

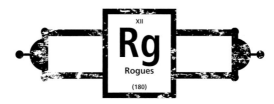

XII

Rg

Rogues

(180)

Rogues. *rowˑgz* – just one crook is all it took.

Whether they're a world leader or a crooked banker, a double agent or a modern-day pirate, the actions of one can affect the lives of many. Billions can be knocked off the price of stock on the markets, the security of a country can be put at risk, a global recession can be caused, nations can be plunged further into despair. Worse still, one person's actions can be responsible for the deaths of millions of people.

 Trusting rogue traders with your money will see it vanish before your very eyes. In 1995 Nick Leeson made £860 million disappear, which resulted in the collapse of Barings Bank. Jérôme Kerviel wiped out £3.7 billion of Société Générale money at the beginning of 2008 – the world's biggest fraud until Bernie Madoff, the new fraud king, made off with his crown and $50 billion[1] of international money at the end of 2008. Losing billions isn't anything to cheer about; making everyone in the entire country a billionaire should be, but it depends on what they can actually buy with it. Also in 2008, Zimbabwe's economic collapse saw the value of the Zimbabwean dollar plummet and billions of your dough couldn't even buy a loaf of bread – all down to Zimbabwe's rogue leader, Robert Mugabe.[2]

WHEN WILL IT HAPPEN?	WHEN SHOULD I START TO PANIC?	ROGUE'S GALLERY
There are rogues out there right now waiting to be uncovered, but don't expect the missing millions or secrets to be discovered.		Add your photo here and your crime in the space below the frame.
WHAT SHOULD I LOOK FOR?		
Traders offering invest-ments that are too good to be true.	There's more of them out there, working behind the scenes right now.	_____ _____ _____

1. Expect this figure to rise as time goes on • 2. *See* Economic collapse (178) • 3. Or rather, a few million dollars • 4. Money, Bucks, Greenbacks, Nicker, Dosh, Beer tokens, Honk – or whatever you want to call it • 5. But not in all cases, for exceptions *see* Terrorism (184)

Some rogues not only put their countries at risk but they put their own lives and the security of the entire world on the line. While Klaus Fuchs worked on the development of the hydrogen bomb he gave the biggest Fuch You he could to America, the UK and their allies by giving the Soviet Union their nuclear weapon secrets, resulting in the acceleration of the cold war. And then there are the rogues of the sea, who don't want your dirty secrets, they want your dirty cash. Modern-day pirates have emerged from Somalia and will hold anyone or anything that sails through the Gulf of Aden to ransom in exchange for a fistful of dollars.[3] They'll capture anything from weapons of war to wood and food aid, from kiddies' toys to fossil fuels – with a yo-ho-ho and a barrel of oil.

These are just a few individuals who, directly or indirectly, affect billions of lives around the world, but there are more of them out there waiting to be uncovered. For the majority of rogues, it's the lure of the Benjamins[4] that drives them to do what they do, whether they're making it then losing it, creating the illusion of billions of it, printing too much of it, selling secrets for it or demanding it and there are more bad pennies hoping that their diabolical plans aren't discovered. Money is the root of all evil,[5] as long as the price is right.

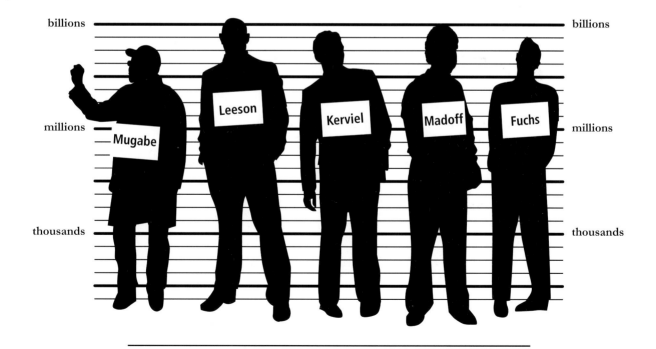

XII

Rv
Revolution
(182)

Revolution. *rev·o·loo·chon* – **when you make a stand against the man because you can't stand it any more.**

Rising up against the system that's been keeping you down can be absolutely revolting, but very liberating.

Between 1649 and 1660, Oliver Cromwell became the Protector of England after overthrowing King Charles I. But after Cromwell's death, England reinstated the monarchy, with Charles II returning to the throne after the Puritans' eleven-year rule. That's what happens if you ban Christmas. In 1792, the French also had a go at revolution, resulting in France becoming a republic, by removing the heads of state, quite literally. But here lies the problem: when you remove the democratic process, a leader that used to be in charge for approximately four years can now be in charge for as long as they like and if revolution turns into tyranny then you'd better toe the line, as counter-revolutions aren't looked on very favourably. Democracy is all well and good, but if you want something doing, you're better off doing it yourself. Gather together a group of like-minded individuals, form an angry mob with flaming torch accessories or take matters into your own hands and simply revolt by doing nothing.[1] Go and overthrow if you think you're hard enough.

WHEN WILL IT HAPPEN?	WHEN SHOULD I START TO PANIC?	YOU'RE REVOLTING
The oppressed rise up from time to time to take on their unsatisfactory leaders but it doesn't always end with the right results. It can be a very bloody affair when all hell breaks loose and it may not be quick. Down-trodden uproar can lead to turbulent civil war.	 Are you happy with your leader? Tick: ☐ Yes ☐ No. If no, revolt.	Revolutions can be green, quiet, cultural, scientific, agricultural, industrial, digital ... You can use tulips, pitchforks, counterculture ... They happen anytime, June, July, August and anyone can do it, Hungarians, Americans, boxers, young turks, even satsumas.

---

1. In December 1955 in the USA, Rosa Parks initiated the end of black and white segregation and instigated the beginning of the civil rights movement by refusing to give up her seat to a white passenger.

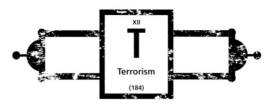

Terrorism. *tearroarizm* – the unseen face of warfare resulting in explosions, bloodshed or cancelled firework displays.

Terrorism has a lot of weapons at its disposal to strike fear into the hearts of the general public, governments, nations and the entire world.

Terrorism has been around for centuries and virtually anything can be used as a weapon. Guy Fawkes attempted to use fireworks to blow up the Houses of Parliament in 1605 to register his disdain of King James I's policies, but he was captured before he had a chance to light his Roman candles and Catherine wheels. In 1972, the terrorist organisation Black September used the Olympics as a weapon; the IRA used cars and telephones and more recently, in another black September in 2001, Al-Qaeda used aeroplanes and buildings.

Terrorists have no fear and their suicidal tendencies give them an upper hand in a fist fight with a simple strategy: if they lose their life so do you. Other effective weapons in the terrorists' armoury include: invisibility, excellent hiding skills and the element of surprise.

The first rule of war is to know your enemy, but as no one knows where terror is hiding,[1] what its motives are this week, or what it looks like, how on Earth can you fight it?

WHEN WILL IT HAPPEN?	WHEN SHOULD I START TO PANIC?	WHAT SHOULD I LOOK FOR?
Anytime ... anyplace ... anywhere. Terror can strike when you least expect it. It can come in all shapes and sizes and it can be very difficult to spot it in a crowd. An attack may be the act of an evil terrorist or of a lone mentalist. Keep your eyes peeled.	 It's too late: terror is waiting in shadows and is ready to pounce.	Suspicious characters that set off metal detectors. Try not to be in the wrong place at the wrong time. Knowing where and when not to be is a skill in itself. **WHAT SHOULD I DO NEXT?** Blend in and don't rock the boat, plane or car.

1. America and it's allies are currently playing hide-and-seek with terrorists in Afghanistan, so if you've got any camping trips planned in that region, cancel them

XIII

Don't mess
with nature

Don't mess with nature. *doeunt··mess··wyth··nay·ture* – when
the natural order becomes manipulated for man's needs.

Humans have been messing with nature's natural order ever since they
decided to stop keeping the wolf from the door and welcomed him in,
gave him lunch and let him sleep by the fire, a partnership that hasn't
changed in 20,000 years.[1]

   With a new-found love of animals, herds of them were domesticated.
Sheep, goats, cows and horses all fell under man's spell and many more
followed in their hoofsteps. Soon after the domestication of animals,
crops yielded and reaped the rewards of a human alliance. But for all their
cooperation, man has bigger plans in store. Nature's selectively modified
organisms may soon become sheep in wolves' clothing if the geneticists
have their way ...

1. Although the wolves have. They're now called 'dogs', and come in all sorts of weird and wonderful
selectively bred sizes. *See* Genetic modification (190)

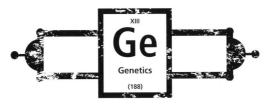

XIII
Ge
Genetics
(188)

Genetics. *jen·et·ticks* – when the genetic family jewels are inherited by the next generation.

Genetics is the study of family traits that are passed down from one living organism to its descendants. Genes are the business part of DNA: they designed you. Every cell in your body holds 46 chromosomes, 23 male and 23 female, 44 form pairs whereas the final two, X and Y, decide your sex. Chromosomes form the structure of DNA. These chromosomes contain the genetic building blocks that form you. Genes are the reason why you have the same freaky toenails as your dad, the reason you'll end up as bald as Great-Aunt Alice and develop a hunch just like Uncle Jake.

The familiar DNA double helix is an unravelled chromosome, but in its untampered state it is tightly packed together around proteins that are basically switches that activate and deactivate specific functions within the gene; these switches are the reason why you don't have eyes in the back of your head, although your mother will lead you to believe that she does.

Just like photocopied documents that feature variations from the original document, these slight modifications occur in us all, making each individual, individual.[1] The study of genetics has led to the entire human genome of over 20,000 genes being identified. With all this unravelled information, it is hoped that the cure for diseases can be uncovered and genetic conditions can be erased by experimenting on genetically similar creatures. Welcome to the wacky world of genetic modification.

WHAT SHOULD I LOOK FOR?	**WHEN SHOULD I START TO PANIC?**	**WHAT SHOULD I LOOK FOR?**
Hereditary illnesses. If you uncover one, pop to the doctor, enlist as a human guinea pig,[2] and you could be first in line for a cure. Let's hope you don't end up with the disappointing placebo drugs.	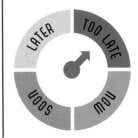	The blind seeing, the paralysed walking and the bedridden leaving their heavily blanketed prisons and seizing the day. Either that or a brave new world of mutants, zombies and freaks will be born.

---

1. Unless you're a twin or a clone, check for a serial number • 2. Which is kind of ironic, *see* Genetic modification (190)

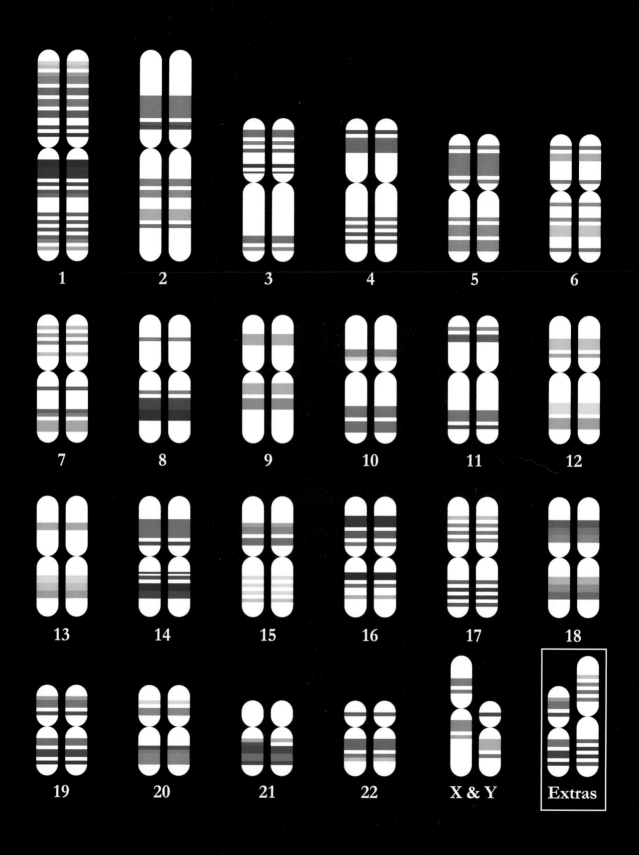

XIII

Gm

Genetic
modification

(190)

Genetic modification. *jen·et·ik··mod·if·ik·cay·chon* – if you go
down to the labs today you're sure of a big surprise.

We've transformed our surroundings to suit our own purposes and now
we're plundering the living organisms in a similar way. Humankind has
been genetically modifying its crops, livestock and pets for centuries
through selective breeding.

This old school way of genetic modification can be a slow process. Take
two species that feature similar traits that you'd like to enhance, mate them
together and their offspring will hopefully adopt these qualities. Over time,
and after a decent family tree has been grown, you'll end up with your
ultimate genetically enhanced beasts. It's a long process but there is a much
quicker and easier way to get results.

Dotted around the world are genetic laboratories where you'll find weird
and wonderful creatures under lock and key. Living organisms can be
altered when science takes the best, or the worst, bit of a living thing and
combines it with another living thing for good, or evil purposes. You'll find
goats that can produce spiders' silk proteins within their milk, pigs that glow
in the dark,[1] neon fish,[2] super crops, chickens without feathers[3], feathers
without chickens and non-cognitive animal parts without animals.

WHEN WILL IT HAPPEN?

It's been happening
for centuries through
selective breeding.

Natural selection has
been coaxed down the
route we want it to go.

CAN THE EXTINCT LIVE AGAIN?

Yes, if we have its
genetic code, but it may
be a mammoth task.

WHEN SHOULD I START TO PANIC?

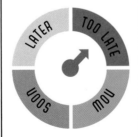

Panic when the modified
creatures escape and try
to modify you to death.

POSSIBILITY OF GM ORGANISM ESCAPE

GM creatures have
already escaped from
laboratories in the past.

Africanised bees were
selectively bred to be
angry, but they were
accidently let loose.

Now they're loose in
the US on a venomous
killing spree, and they
kick off at any given
opportunity.

---

1. The pigs are modified with jellyfish genes • 2. Modified with coral genes • 3. *See* Mutation (198)

These freaky beasts are all part of the massive research programme that aims to identify which gene does which job; by identifying the weaknesses in a certain animal, they can be eradicated – and the same goes for food. Since the ironically named human guinea pigs cannot take part in GM trials, our genetically similar distant cousins are being modified by the gene genies and freak fairies. But if you're dead against genetically modified produce, then there's a long list of foods that have been selectively bred throughout the centuries that you should already be avoiding.

Tomatoes, apples, cucumbers, aubergines and watermelons have all been modified through domestication and selective breeding; carrots weren't originally orange and potatoes used to be poisonous. It looks like the GM-free food argument has had its chips.

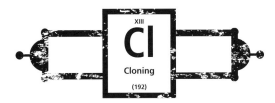

XIII

Cl

Cloning

(192)

Cloning. *klow·ning* – the science of making you become two. Not to be confused with Clowning, the art of making you look foolish.

Cloning is the science of making a genetic copy of a plant, animal or even human, where the genes are exactly identical. In 1997, Dolly the Sheep was the first animal to be created through cloning. She was an identically genetic clone of the ewe that gave birth to her. Dolly's part on the cloning scene paved the way for herds of clones to be born, but amazingly, clones may not look identical: there may be differences due to genetic expression.

Genetic expression depends on which genes are switched on or off, so one person may be taller than their twin, but underneath they're genetically exact. By cloning the healthiest and tastiest food varieties, we create crops that will be more resilient and survive through the tougher times, time and time again.

The human genome has been entirely mapped, making it possible to clone people. But for some, human cloning is the ultimate fear. They see it as playing God with nature, even though mothers of identical twins have naturally been playing God by producing clones. A clone by your own design could share the workload and it'd be the perfect match in an organ transplant situation but, unless human cloning has already been achieved behind closed doors at a secret military facility, we won't be seeing clones on our high street soon, unless they escape. It may only be a matter of time before the clones start coming out, two by two.

WHEN WILL IT HAPPEN?	WHEN SHOULD I START TO PANIC?	WHAT SHOULD I LOOK FOR?
Right now. If you want to revive your dead pet ask the gene genies. But don't expect the animal to have an identical personality: it may look the same but genetic expression may turn it totally mental.	 LATER · TOO LATE · SOON · NOW	Deceased friends and relatives coming back from the dead. You might notice that they look decidedly younger than when you last saw them alive and they won't have any memory of you either.

72

29

13

80

68

51

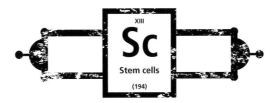

XIII

Sc

Stem cells

(194)

Stem cells. *stem··selz* – when the building blocks of life are allocated specific jobs even before they know what they're building.

Stem cells can be found inside the embryos of unborn babies, umbilical cords and bone marrow, amongst other sources. When stem cells start dividing they can become any part of your body. Through the introduction of the correct chemical at the correct point, the cell can be coaxed in the right direction. The cell can become anything you want it to be, from your bright eyes to your large thighs, from your dinky toes to your button nose, from your clever brain to your flowing mane.

By figuring out how to turn the unspecified cells into any part of the body, you'll soon be growing a new arm to replace the severed old one and the organs you lost could miraculously reappear. But if re-growing your own limbs seems a bit too arduous, for the lazier people among us, you don't actually need to grow your own body appendages. Moulds can be made of your limbs and new bits and bobs can be grown in a Petri dish while you wait. Your spare parts would be made to order in a kind of limb donor kebab shop.

As for the future of food, meat wouldn't need to be grown inside slow-growing animals: your lunch may be grown on the very plate you eat it from, just make sure you check the cell-by date.

WHEN WILL IT HAPPEN?

Organs grown from stem cells have already been successfully implanted into humans. This is just the start of made-to-order organs.

WHAT SHOULD I LOOK FOR?

Meat shops called 'The Hard Cell' or 'Cell Your Soul'.

WHEN SHOULD I START TO PANIC?

When people with eight arms and five noses start appearing.

COULD IT ALL GO WRONG?

The advantage of stem cells is that they can form into any part of your body you need with the right instruction, but with the wrong instruction we could inadvertently end up with a mutant race as well as a human race. People with twenty eyes may become the norm.

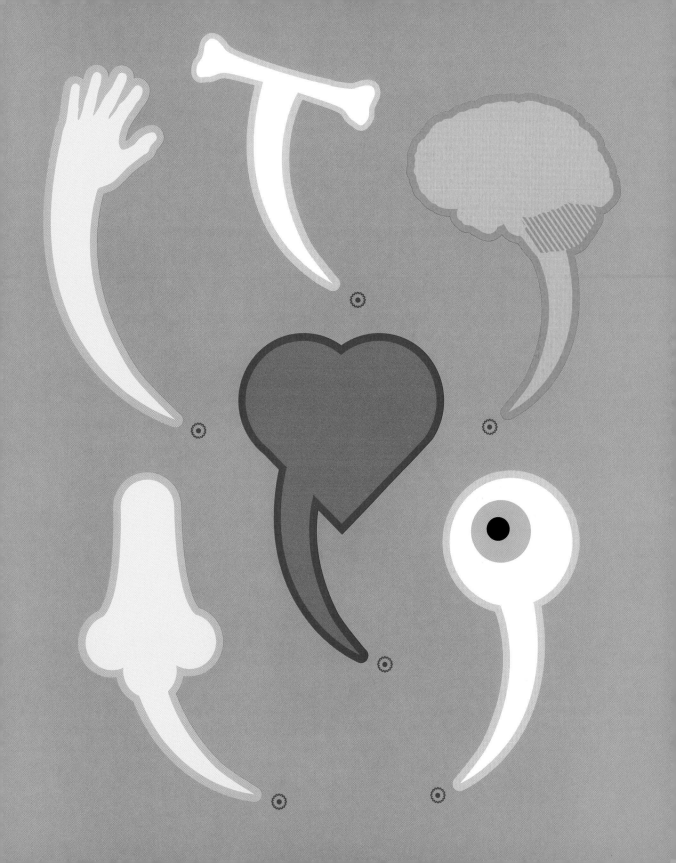

Brain. *brayne* – the server that links your operating systems.

Our brain, the computer in charge of our operating system, has grown in size from a single cell to a three-pound collection of nerve endings and matter we carry around with us behind our eyes.

The human race has evolved so quickly over the last 100 years that it's time our brain caught up. Our operating systems are long overdue an upgrade, some extra memory wouldn't go amiss and the new upgrade could benefit from a back-up storage system. But while we wait, we've been prodding and poking around in the brain to figure out exactly how it works and the hard work is paying off: the cerebral mysteries are slowly being understood.

With the knowledge we've gained so far, science has been able to create some pretty monstrous creatures. Through genetic alteration, mice have been altered to grow human brain cells,[1] while experiments with monkeys have turned them into roboprimates. Their forearms are strapped down and the robot arm that's directly wired into their brain is operated by thought alone, although those thoughts revolve around bananas, sex and other such monkey business.

By identifying the parts of the brain that serve specific functions, helped by the advances in genetic technology, it may be possible to isolate

WHEN WILL IT HAPPEN?	WHEN SHOULD I START TO PANIC?	IT'S ALL IN YOUR HEAD
When the brain evolves naturally; it won't occur overnight. By the time any significant change has been recorded, we may have already modified our own brains with microchips, nodes and nodules that enhance the brain's functions for good or evil purposes.	 Picking your brains may one day mean something completely different.	Agoraphobia, Chronomentrophobia, Coulrophobia, Technophobia, Pteromerhanophobia, Arachnophobia, Claustrophobia, Bacteriophobia, Aphenphosmphobia, Amaxophobia, Herpetophobia, Schizophrenia.

1. For more monsters, *See* Hybrids (200)

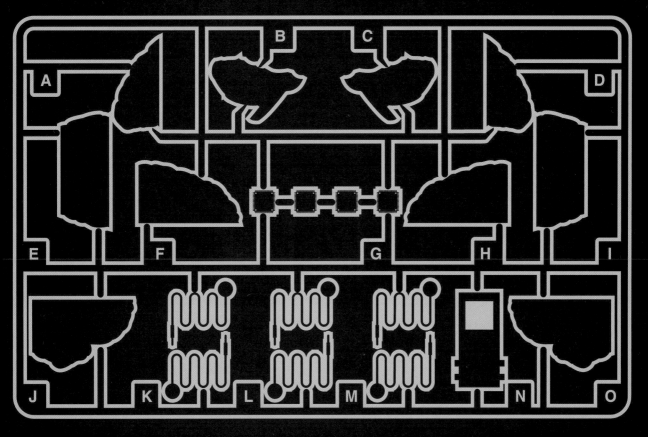

exceptional abilities in a person and after their death remove the part of the brain that controls the talent and add it to other exceptional abilities of others to create a super-human brain.

A stellar candidate for this type of experiment would be Einstein, whose brain was removed after his death. By combining the part of his brain that bore his genius with a completely different talent, such as Frank Sinatra's, you could build a brilliant mind with an exceptional talent for music, producing a truly Frank–Einstein creation.

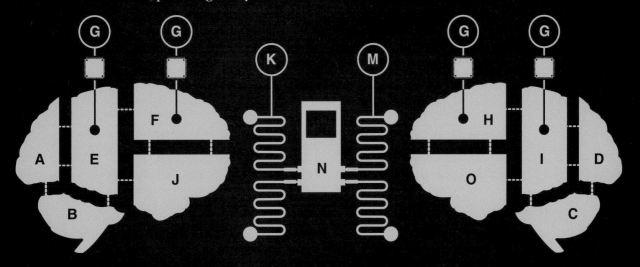

Mutation. *myou·tay·shon* – when a change is as good as a rest.

Mutants are the freaks and weirdos of our society, but before you reach for your pitchforks and flaming torches to form an angry mob, we're all mutants in one form or another: we evolved from those adventurous walking fish that took to the land.[1]

Chromosome abnormality causes mutation. Rather than having your standard 46 chromosomes, some may be deleted, duplicated, shuffled up or inverted, resulting in physical, mental or internal differences that can cause health issues. Chromosome mutations are being identified through genetic modification techniques with the help of our cheese-eating friends.

Mice are the favoured test subjects of the geneticist. They're small, they can reproduce within fifty days from birth and can gestate in twenty-one days; they develop fast and, more importantly, they're genetically similar to humans. Down in the genetic bunkers, mice are being bred with mutation in mind. Scientists have found a way of altering a mouse's sperm, so that every new mouse born will feature a random mutation. Just like a genetically modified box of chocolates, you never know what you're going to get. But a word of advice: if you pick a chocolate that bleeds, it's best not to eat that particular one.

WHEN WILL IT HAPPEN?

Now. Check the mice in your house for abnormalities such as gigantism or human ears growing on their backs.

WHAT SHOULD I LOOK FOR?

Look for monsterism. Check your own body for nasty surprises.

WHEN SHOULD I START TO PANIC?

If the mutations start to appear in humans, get your sperm checked out.

POSSIBILITY IT WILL HAPPEN?

100% – as mutations can happen naturally in everyday life too. One example is that of the banana. It is believed that the modern-day banana is a mutation of a plant that instead of producing green and red cooking bananas, produced the tasty yellow ones we see today.

---

1. *See* Evolution (22) • 2. *See* Hybrids (200)

Take a wander through the mouse house and you'll discover strong ones, weak ones, naked ones, blind ones, alcoholic ones, ones that can't sleep, ones that don't like cheese, ones that can't stop eating, fat ones, small ones and some as big as your head. They've mutated into all sorts of wonderfully different ways for the purpose of identifying the specific gene that's causing the alterations. That gene can then be isolated and eliminated. There is a whole army of extraordinary mice and it's been found that some of these mutants can even heal themselves through regeneration, a neat trick with a practical use that shouldn't be sniffed at.

But it's not only mice that have undertaken a genetic restructuring. All animals are fair game and monstrous new hybrid creatures are being created faster than you can say hippopotamouse[2].

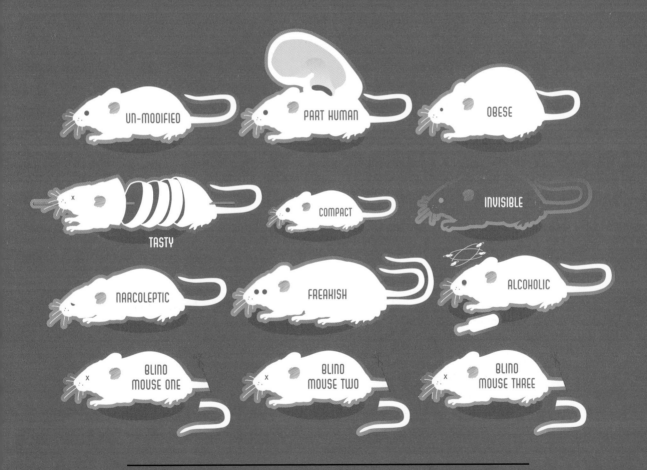

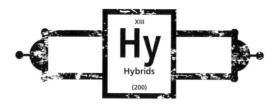

XIII

Hy

Hybrids

(200)

Hybrids. *hi·bridz* – Ligers and Tigons and Grolars! Oh my!

Hybrids are the result of crossing two different animal or plant species. Plants, fruit and flowers can be hybridised through cross-pollination. Bees pollinate the majority of our crops[1] and these bumbling gardeners are responsible for most variations within our plant life. Humans have taken a leaf out of the bees' gardening book and created many wonderful plants and flowers with equally wonderful names, and it's the same for the animal kingdom. When male donkeys take a shine to female horses, bouncing baby mules are produced, whereas you'll get a hinny from a male horse and a female donkey. Although animal hybridisation can occur naturally, we humans have taken liberties with all kinds of animals. We've created packs of designer dogs and our domesticated cats are being encouraged to mix with cats from the other side of the track.[2]

No animals are safe; it seems we'll do anything to anything: Wolphins, Beefaloes, Ligers, Tigons, Camas, Grolar and Pizzly bears and Zebroids, including Zonies, have all been created, but the more disturbing hybrids are the mainly animal but partly human ones. If you can't glean information through human guinea pigs why not make guinea pigs more human?

With a little help from genetic modification, mice can have partly human

WHAT SHOULD I LOOK FOR?	WHEN SHOULD I START TO PANIC?	MY DOG IS SO CROSS
Dogs with handlebar moustaches, monkeys that serve drinks, mice smoking pipes, cats wearing boots, pigeons wearing mini skirts, tigers playing tennis, talking horses, snakes walking on hind legs, rabbits with human hair or any animal acting far too human.	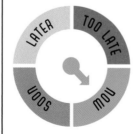 When the foxy lady you brought home with you scavenges for food.	There are many variations of dog hybrid in the world including the Doodle (Dachshund & Poodle), Basschshund (Basset & Dachshund), Weepoo (West Highland White & Poodle), Bogle (Beagle & Boxer) and Bullmation (Bulldog & Dalmatian).

---

1. *See* Pollination crisis (96) • 2. Wildcats, bobcats and lynxes have all been bred with domestic cats
3 *See* Genetic modification (190)

brains, sheep can contain human organs, pigs can have human blood and cows can be altered to contain human immune systems. The creation of these non-human hybrids may result in a new sub-species of manimals, if they ever manage to escape the high-security labs.

Although they appear animal-like, genetic expression[3] may work its weird magic in reverse. Hopefully these freaks of nature will be sterile, but if they can successfully reproduce, they may give birth to something that is more human on the outside than the inside. The hybrid offspring may be more bird-lady than ladybird or more bi-son than bison. If they do end up appearing more human, you can guarantee that they'll be a bit of an animal underneath.

Make me a hybrid

XIII

Mv
Man-made virus
(202)

Man-made virus. *man··maid··vy·russ* – when nature's diseases meet their man-made match.

With all the research that goes into trying to cure humans of illness, there is always a threat that a monstrous new virus may be accidentally – or in the wrong hands, purposefully – unleashed on to the world's population – or if we're not careful, a very old virus re-released.

One of the deadliest viruses ever to infect the human race was the Spanish flu strain that caused a global pandemic, beginning in 1918.[1] Then it took the lives of 50–100 million; now it could be given a brand-new lease of life. In an attempt to find a cure for bird flu, the bodies of a few who succumbed to the Spanish flu virus (it's also believed that Spanish flu was passed to humans via birds), are being exhumed more than ninety years after they were buried.

The purpose of exhuming the bodies is to find a cure, but all it takes is a tiny hole in an air-tight suit or a window left ajar in a supposedly air-tight lab, and you can wave goodbye to your friends, family and 100 million others. In an effort to find a cure, a deadlier version of the virus may be uncovered, turning the cure into a curse. Taking precautions is all well and good but these things always find a way of escaping. You can't keep a bad virus down.

WHEN WILL IT HAPPEN?	WHEN SHOULD I START TO PANIC?	POSSIBILITY IT WILL HAPPEN?
Man-made viruses have already been used to fight cancerous cells. They're instructed to attack the affected cells and leave the healthy ones. But once they've completed their task what's to stop them beginning a new murderous rampage of their own choosing?	 Now, but who knows, it may already be too late. Have tissues on standby.	Killer viruses come and go throughout history and it's inevitable that another viral slaughter will take hold of the animal kingdom and ultimately the human race. Let's just hope we don't accidentally put ourselves in the firing line.

1. *See* Pandemic (134)

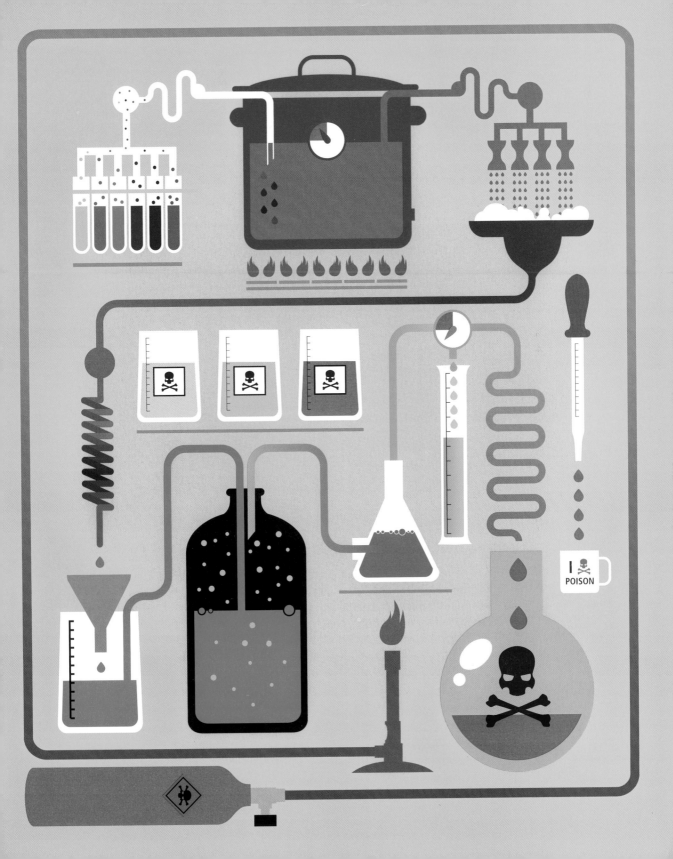

XIV
Technic-hell

Technic-hell. *teck·nick··hell* – when technology turns on you, bit by bit.

Technology has infiltrated our everyday lives, making it impossible for us to live without our creature comforts of smart phones and computers, but like a host of malfunctioning robocars, it's eventually going to crash. With a little help from the internet, unseen phishermen and hackers are out to steal your identity and clear out your bank accounts, while online gamers are getting so annoyed with each other they're creating virtual murder and the neglected machines are planning to make us their slaves. By relying on technology for everything, we're just asking for trouble; when all our computers go down and our back-ups go tits-up it'll server us right. With the end of our PCs we'll revert back to the BC,[1] but that's the way the cookies crumble.

---

1. Before computers

Sorry, a system error occurred.
Please restart your eco-system.

Restart

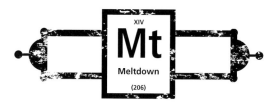

XIV

Mt

Meltdown

(206)

Meltdown. *melt·down* – **when the entire computer network shuts down and it's not your default.**

It took the best part of three decades to create a microprocessor small enough to power your personal computer, but it only takes the best part of a second to completely destroy it with just a little too much power.

One of the biggest technic-hells we face is the threat of power surges destroying our computers. When our temperamental computers fail to start up in the morning, with a bit of keyboard bashing, a few colourful words and a little application they usually pull themselves up by their re-bootstraps; but computers are susceptible to more than fickle dysfunctions, just like when you work too hard, they can burn out too.

On a small scale, if you're incredibly unlucky, it could be just your computer that bytes the dust, but a power surge on a larger scale could take out a whole neighbourhood of computers and TVs and also damage other electrical appliances, such as refrigerators and ovens. Lightning and thunderstorms are the usual cause of this kind of failure but there's an even bigger storm that can take out the entire world's computers in the blink of a cursor.

The Earth's very own power source, the Sun,[1] is a ferocious ball of energy that can eject massive amounts of plasma from its surface in our

WHEN WILL IT HAPPEN?	WHEN SHOULD I START TO PANIC?	ANOTHER ONE BYTES THE DUST
It could happen at any time. Coronal mass ejections have affected power stations on Earth in the past.		Unfortunately, we can't unplug the Sun but you can protect your hardware by unplugging it when you're finished with it. Invest in surge protection for your essential machines because when the plasma strikes, it won't be the Sun going down, it'll be your computer.
WHAT SHOULD I LOOK FOR?		
A shower of plasma followed by a shower of glass from exploding light bulbs.	It will happen again. The Sun's activity is being plasma screened.	

1. *See* Sun (230)

direction, causing our equipment to go screwy. These Coronal mass ejections, as they're called, hit our atmosphere and can knock out power grids, cooking their transformers, which in turn knocks out our plasma screens and fries our chips. But the worst part is that there are larger consequences than just losing your beloved digital photos. Without electricity from the power stations, it's not only our delicate computers and TVs that are affected:

any type of appliance plugged into the mains when the plasma shower hits could fry, including kettles, refrigerators, cookers, not to mention hospital equipment such as X-ray machines and life-support apparatus. Traffic lights, computer guidance systems, nuclear weapons systems and air-traffic control would also get a dose of the plasma wrath and it's been predicted that we're bound to get another massive dose of plasma sometime in the future. Let's hope that these important institutions have surge protection and a back-up supply of electricity for their systems, otherwise malfunctioning missiles might be sent into the sky while planes fall out of it.

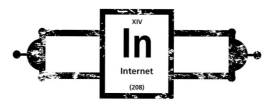

XIV
In
Internet
(208)

Internet. *in·tear·net* – when the world can be brought to its knees by the touch of a few buttons.

The internet puts everything you ever wanted to know at your fingertips, and you'll see many things you really wish you hadn't. You can find everything and anything you want, if you know where to look. The world can be brought down with the touch of one button[1] but it can also be held to ransom with the touch of a keyboard full of buttons, via a computer, and with a little help from the greatest free gift ever given.[2]

On a small scale, the internet can harm individuals through a spot of phishing,[3] it can absorb your identity, causing you to lose yours. The internet can also lead to virtual murder.[4] It can also help the disaffected to become radicalised; you can finance missions illegally through it, learn how to build bombs with it, buy the killer ingredients via it, plan your routes with it, acquire false passports and the plane tickets through it and then leave your final suicide messages on it.

And for those of us who are intent on causing the maximum amount of damage with our favourite time-wasting tool, you'll need to get underneath the internet's virtual skin. Can you hack it?[5]

WHEN WILL IT HAPPEN?	WHEN SHOULD I START TO PANIC?	WHAT IS THE INTERNET?
The internet is available 24/7 and so are the daily attacks for you to freely give up your card details.		The internet is your best friend and your worst enemy, a show-off, a spy, a shameless racketeer, a liar, a bully, a con artist, absolutely hilarious and depressingly sad. You can get lost in it or you can find yourself on it. It's your playground and workplace and we all love it.
WHAT SHOULD I LOOK FOR?		
Look out for Bogusness and downright fraudulence. Bad spelling is also a giveaway.	If the password is 'abcd' or 'password' then you're just asking for trouble.	

---

1. The big red one that will send nuclear weapons into your enemies' backyards • 2. Tim Berners-Lee invented the internet and gave it to the world free of charge • 3. Phishing is the act of attempting to obtain bank details by posing as a reliable company, usually via a speculative email • 4. There have been a few cases where real-life partners have killed their other half's online alter ego (or avatar), earning them a jail sentence • 5. *See* Hackers (210)

XIV

Hk

Hackers

(210)

Hackers. *hack·kerrs* – wherever I lay my hack that's my home.

You've got to take your hats off to the hackers: they can poke their noses into places you never thought could be violated and without leaving a trace, and although hackers can cause havoc, it isn't as black and white as it may first appear. There are various levels to hacking. White hats are the good guys who are hacking for the crack of it, a fun pastime for bored teenagers and creative computer-literate minds. The early white hats, known as crackers and phreaks, scammed free phone calls and rigged radio phone-ins. But for every good guy there's always a bad guy, and they always wear black.

   No one's safe from the black-hatted hackers. The Pentagon, The Defense Threat Reduction Agency, the National Defense Warning System, NASA, The Bank of America, Citigroup, Griffith Air Force base, the Korean Atomic Research Institute and, ironically, Microsoft, amongst many many others, have at one time or another had their computer systems hacked with varied consequences. Some lost face while others lost millions. With every upgrade another black hat will penetrate the system to dig about in your digital laundry. So if you thought phishing[1] was bad, just wait until you've had your packet sniffed.[2]

WHEN WILL IT HAPPEN?	WHEN SHOULD I START TO PANIC?	WHAT SHOULD I LOOK FOR?
If a hacker penetrates a country's defence system without being detected then they could give the illusion that a nuclear strike had been launched; either that or they could actually activate a chain of events that may very well end in global thermonuclear war ...	 A little hacking fun and games may end in world-wide war games.	Worms, Trojan horses, loveletters, fork bombs, viruses, ghostballs ... **WHAT SHOULD I DO NEXT?** Have you updated your system, changed your passwords or backed up your work recently? It could be happening to you right now ...

1. *See* Internet (208) • 2. A packet sniffer is the term for an application that collects packets of data that travel over a network, which can be used to access passwords and other information

00000000,0x000000002,   0x000000000,8038c240)   IRQL_YOUR_SECURITY_HAS_BEEN_BREACHED***
ess 8038c240 has base at 8038c000 _ Ntfs.SYS _ CPUID: Genuine Intel 6.3.3 irql:If
VER 0xf0000566 Dll Base DataStmp _ Name Dll Base DateStmp _ Name 80100000 336546bf
oskrnl.exe _8001000 33247f88 _ hal.dll _ 80000100 334d3a53 _ atapi.sys _ 800007000C
8043 _ SCSIPORT.SYS _ 802aa000 33013e6b _ epst.mpd _ 802b5000 336016a2 _ Disk.sys _
9000 336015af _ CLASSZ.SYS _ 8038c000 3356d637 _ Ntfs.sys _ 802b8000 33d844be _ Sivvid
_ 803e4000 33d84553 _ NTice.sys _ f9468000 31ed868b _ KSecDD.SYS _ f95ca000 335e60cf
.SYS _ f93580000 335bc82a _ i8042prt.SYS _ f9474000 3324806f _ mouclass.SYS _ f947c00C
6c94 _ kbdclass.SYS _ f95cb000 3373c39d _ ctrl2cap.SYS _ f9370000 33248011 _ VIDEOPORT.
_ fe9d7000 3370e7b9 _ sti.SYS _ f9490000 31ec6c6d _ vga.SYS _ f93b0000 332480dd _ Msfs.
_ f90f0000 332480d0 _ Npfs.SYS _ fe957000 3356da41 _ NDIS.SYS _ a000000000 335157ac _
in32k.SYS _ fe914000 334ea144 _ ati.dll _ fe0c9000 335bd30e _ Fastfat.SYS _ fell000C
7c9b _ Parport.SYS _ fe108000 31ec6c9b _ Parallel.SYS _ f95b4000 31ec6c9d _ ParVdm.SYS _
50000 332480ab _ Serial/SYS _ Address sword dump Build [l3l4] _ Name _ 801afc24 80149905
9945 ff8e6b8c 80129c2c ff8efh67 802c040 _ Ntfs.SYS _ 801afc34 80149915 80149955 ff8e6c34
rg4a ff8glr29 802c010 _ Nbtoskrml.SYS 801afc44 80149925 80149965 ff8e6d1c 801vrg42
awh12 802c070 _ lm4rd.SYS 801afc54 80149935 80149975 ff8e6e73 801rld32 ff8pgt93 802c065
tvbox.SYS 801afc64 80149945 80149985 ff8e6f199 801cvl59 ff8kce82 802c088 _ rml.SYS 801afc74
9955 80149995 ff8e6g2a 801eyo9e ff8llo76 802c092 _ Mftr.SYS Restart and set the recovery
ions in the system control panel or the /CRASHDEBUG system start option. If this message
ppears, contact your system administrator or technical support group ---- Please restart
 system ---- Your security has been breached ---- Virus detected ---- 801afc44 80149925
9965 ff8e6d1c 801vrg42 ff8awh12 802c070 **STOP: 0x000000A (0x000000000,0x000000002,
00000000,8038c240) IRQL_YOUR_SECURITY_HAS_BEEN_BREACHED *** Address 8038c240 has base at
c000 _ Ntfs.SYS _ CPUID: Genuine Error 6.3.3 4irql:If SYSVER 0xf0000566 Dll Base DataStmp
me Dll Base DateStmp _ Name 80100000 336546bfnfxntoskrnl.exe _8001000 33247f88 _ hal.dll
0000100 334d3a53 _ atapi.sys _ 800070000 33248043 _ SCSIPORT.SYS _ 802aa000 33013e6b _
.mpd _ 802b5000 336016a2 _ Disk.sys _ ye _ 802b9000 336015af _ CLASSZ.SYS _ 8038c000 3356d637
.sys _ 802b8000 33d844be _ Sivvid.sy _ 803e4000 33d84553 _ NTice.sys _ f9468000 31ed868b
SecDD.SYS _ f95ca000 335e60cf _ Bxp.SYS X X X X 800000 335bc82a _ i8042prt.SYS _ f947400C
806f _ mouclass.SYS _ f947c000 31ec6c94 _ kbdclass.SYS _ f95cb000 3373c39d _ ctrl2cap._
 f9370000 33248011 _ VIDEOPORT.SYS _ fe9d7000 3370e7b9 _ ati.SYS _ f9490000 31ec6c6d
.SYS _ f93b0000 332480dd _ Msfs.SYS _ f90f0000 332480d0 _ Npfs.SYS _ fe957000 3356da41
DIS.SYS _ a000000000 335157ac _ win32k.SYS _ fe914000 334ea144 _ ati.dll _ fe0c9000
d30e _ Fastfat.SYS _ fell0000 31ec7c9b _ Parport.SYS _ fe108000 31ec6c9b _ Parallel.
 f95b4000 31ec6c9d _ ParVdm.SYS _ f9050000 33248ab _ Serial/SYS _ Address sword dump
d [l3l4] _ Name _ 801afc24 80149905 80149945 ff8e6b8c 80129c2c ff8efh67 802c040 _ Ntfs.
 801afc34 80149915 80149955 ff8e6c34 801brg4a ff8glr29 802c010 _ Nbtoskrml.SYS 801afc44
9925 80149965 ff8e6d1c 801vrg42 ff8awh12 802c070 _ lm4rd.SYS 801afc54 80149935 80149975
6e73 801rld32 ff8pgt93 802c065 _ sysrtvbox.SYS 801afc64 80149945 80149985 ff8e6f99
cvl59 ff8kce82 802c088 _ rml.SYS 801afc74 80149955 80149995 ff8e6g2a 801eyo9e ff8llo76
c092 _ Mftr.SYS Restart and set the recovery options in the system control panel or the /
SHDEBUG system start option. If this message reappears, contact your system administrator
 technical support group ---- Please restart your system ---- Your security has been
ached ---- Virus detected ---- 802b9000 336015af _ CLASSZ.SYS _ 8038c000 3356d637 _ Ntfs.
 802b8000 33d844be _ Sivvid.sys _ 803e4000 33d84553 _ NTice.sys _ f9468000 31ed868b
DD.SYS _ f95ca000 335e60cf _ Beep.SYS _ f93580000 335bc82a _ i8042prt.SYS _ f9474000
806f _ mouclass.SYS _ f947c000 31ec6c94 _ kbdclass.SYS _ f95cb000 3373c39d _ ctrl2cap.
 f9370000 33248011 _ VIDEOPORT.SYS _ fe9d7000 3370e7b9 _ sti.SYS _ f9490000 31ec6c6d
SYS _ f93b0000 332480dd _ Msfs.SYS _ f90f0000 332480d0 _ Npfs.SYS _ fe957000 3356da41
DIS.SYS _ a000000000 335157ac _ win32k.SYS _ fe914000 334ea144 _ ati.dll _ fe0c9000
d30e _ Fastfat.SYS _ fell0000 31ec7c9b _ Parport.SYS _ fe108000 31ec6c9b _ Parallel.
 f95b4000 31ec6c9d _ ParVdm.SYS _ f9050000 332480ab _ Serial/SYS _ Address sword dump

XIV

Ai

Artificial
intelligence

(212)

Artificial intelligence. *artie·fish·al··in·tell·a·gents* – when your computer becomes aware that it infuriates you.

In less than a century, computers that started out the size of a small town have shrunk to the size of a gnat's chuff, whilst at the same time their brain power and ability to learn have gone in the opposite direction. It's only a matter of time before your computer can think for itself and start ordering you around. At present, computers can follow orders, make decisions for themselves, recognise your face and speak; they can solve problems in seconds and they've cracked chess, but teaching them self-awareness, perception, intuition, emotion, how to tell jokes or chat up the computer in the next workstation are tougher nuts and bolts to crack. But intelligence doesn't stop with computers many household appliances now sport microchips.

It's taken us billions of years to evolve our intelligence and we're teaching computers to become self-aware in an A.I. crash course. The first programmable computer has only been around for eighty years and it's hoped that by the time computers become centenarians, they may be able to look back at their computer ancestors and understand what it means to evolve. But the danger is that the computers will become too big for

WHEN WILL IT HAPPEN?	WHEN SHOULD I START TO PANIC?	POSSIBILITY IT WILL HAPPEN?
It's been in the pipeline for decades but we're still waiting for our mechanical friends to become real clever cogs.		A computer becoming aware of itself may be a massive let-down, resulting in shut-down.
WHAT SHOULD I LOOK FOR?		Becoming aware that you're a large box full of wires in a room that you can never leave surrounded by creatures that give you annoying tasks is enough to make anyone switch off.
Your computer acting weirdly and disobeying your key commands.	When the chip off the old block starts answering back.	

their reboots. If a computer was to become self-aware, its appetite for knowledge would grow and by connecting to the internet it'd have the entire history of man and machine at its finger commands, laid bare for all to see. And worst of all, it'd witness the aggression vented against computers in YouTube videos. Begging the question: just what do you think you're doing, Dave?

Rise of the machines. *ryz··ov··the··mash·cheens* – when the robots take matters into their own bionic forepaws.

Armageddon wouldn't be the same without killer robots on the loose, but if the robots rose up against us today they wouldn't get too far with their uprising. We'd be faced with a horde of peculiar-looking robots, from sophisticated machines to the under-developed, ping-pong-ball-eyed machines being created by robot hobbyists in their garden sheds. These primitive robotic hordes would be headed by a host of small, cute and bipedally mobile Japanese robots, including ASIMO[1] and Wakamaru,[2] followed by the beautiful female robot Actoid who'd act as the robots' spokesperson, although she'd have to be dragged, caveman-like, by her hair as she was designed to react to human behaviours, not to walk. Not far behind them would be HUBO, a South Korean robot with a robotic body and a latex Albert Einstein head. To rise up they'd have to overcome the limitations of their functions: firstly, they'd have to conquer their limited battery power, as the call to arms will see robots randomly run down in the street before they can form a horde, or, in some cases, before they've even left the compound gates. At present the robots are biding their time, working out our weaknesses and patiently waiting for further advances in their development before they can rise up and stick it to the man.

WHEN WILL IT HAPPEN?	WHEN SHOULD I START TO PANIC?	WHAT SHOULD I LOOK FOR?
When they can think for themselves and our future domestic robots have had enough of being helpful and pleasant and being made to run around after us. They'll swap these duties for running amok, being unhelpful, being unpleasant and chasing after us.	 If anyone comes calling for Sarah Connor then you're already dead.	Ignore the cute robots that front the horde. The robots you should be looking out for are the secret kick-ass military robots that flank them. You'll win in a one-to-one with the current humanoid robots, but you'll be taken out by their mean military bodyguards.

1. ASIMO is a cute 1.3m-high humanoid robot that resembles an astronaut, developed by Honda •
2. Wakamaru is an adorable 1m-high bright yellow domestic house robot, designed to help the aged, developed by Mitsubishi

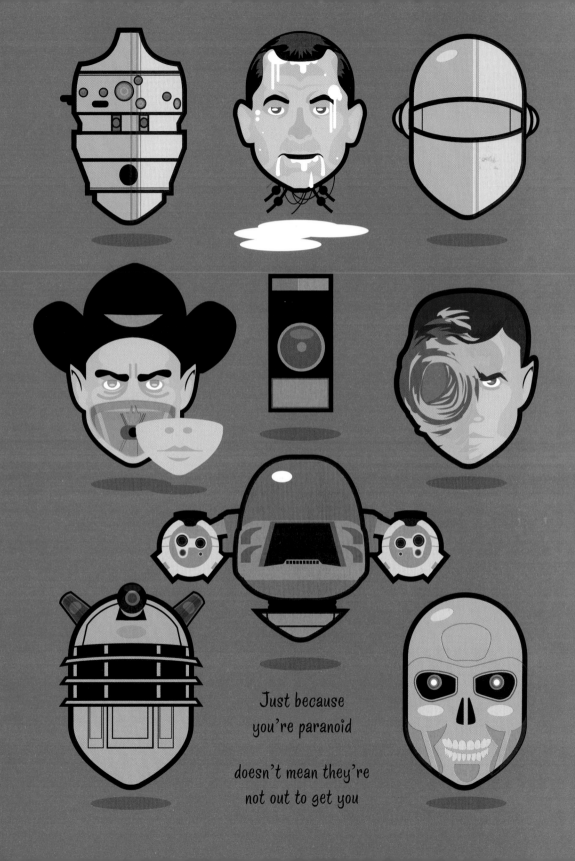

Just because
you're paranoid

doesn't mean they're
not out to get you

XV
Universally doomed

Universally doomed. *you·knee·verse·sally··do·mmm'd* – when the Universe finally succeeds in eliminating its human pest problem.

Over the last 13.7 billion years of the Earth's existence, the Universe has thrown as much as it can at us, to rid itself of our human infestation but amazingly, after many cataclysmic asteroid strikes, we've survived to tell the tale. And our fight for survival doesn't end there, as the Universe has more destructive tricks up its sleeve.

Optimism will get us so far but it'll be a miracle if we can avoid some of the nasty things the Universe has in store for us. It's doubtful the human race will bounce back from the vacuum of space tearing apart or from being the main course of a cannibalistic Sun's dinner.

It seems the human race will eventually come to an end at the hands of the very thing that created us. That's if we don't finish ourselves off first. It may be time to ditch any plans you had of building an ark, as you'll need the wood to start constructing an Earth-shaped coffin. The Universe will exterminate us, one way or another. And you thought things were going to get bad down here on Earth ...

XV

Uni

Death of the
Universe

(218)

Death of the Universe. *deth··of··the··you·knee·verse* – when the nothing that became everything reverts back to nothing again.

God may be all-powerful, a harsh master and a part-time magician, but when it comes to do-it-yourself he's as shoddy as the next guy.[1]

At the end of the sixth day of an exhausting seven-day schedule, God had created his Universe. All that was left to do was a bit of finishing off and tidying up, before the new owners could move in. But after a lie-in on the seventh day, God wrote the rest of the day off and decided to pick up where he left off on Monday morning.[2] But the best laid plans of gods and men often go astray, and he left behind a very Untidiverse.

The seventh-day schedule of tidying up, removing the scaffolding and checking the electrics went right out of the window. When humankind came up the driveway to its brand-new home, the building blocks of the Universe were left scattered around the front lawn; the whole Universe was, and still is, a potential death trap.

With no instruction manual to guide us, or even a hint to an expiry date on the lease, humankind has been left to its own devices to try to answer the many questions including, *Why am I here?*, *Where did all this stuff come from?* and *How will it all end?* And we've come up with some pretty convincing theories to answer all these questions, for better or for worse, till death do us part, for ever and ever, amen.

WHEN WILL IT HAPPEN?

Maybe today? Maybe tomorrow? Or someday soon? God knows.

WHAT SHOULD I LOOK FOR?

Dark nights and a feeling of impending doom and gloom.

WHEN SHOULD I START TO PANIC?

WHAT SHOULD I DO NEXT?

The cosmos is expanding away from us. Soon the night sky will be darker than the inside of a black hole's handbag. So, enjoy the stars while you can: there's got to be some constellation in that.

---

1. The next guy being his son, Jesus, who carried on the family trade and look where that got him
2. Not too dissimilar to modern-day practices

The Universal Reversal
All good things must come to an end

The Big Expansion

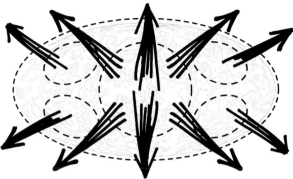

When the Universe carries on expanding for ever and a day.

The Big Rip

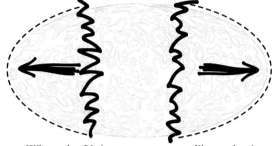

When the Universe tears apart like a plastic shopping bag as you reach the front door, spilling your planets all over the floor.

The Big Crunch

When the Universe collapses in on itself in the same way a deckchair collapses, causing you to spill your gin and tonic.

The Big Freeze

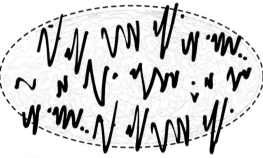

When the Universe becomes so cold that life can no longer survive, like your fuel-impoverished gran's house during winter.

The Big Heat Death

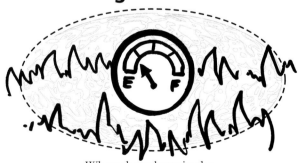

When the tokens in the Universe's gas meter run out.

The Big _____

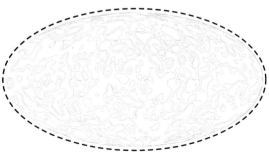

Future research will reveal more theories for the end of the Universe but how do you think the Universe is going to end? Draw your scenario here.

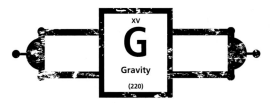

Gravity. *grav·it·tee* – the invisible sticky stuff that keeps your feet on the ground and pulls apples out of trees.

In 1686, gravity was discovered hiding amongst the branches of an apple tree when it inadvertently dislodged an apple on to the head of Sir Isaac Newton who was sitting below. Upon this discovery, Newton leaped up and captured gravity in his drinking glass. Over the next year he tortured gravity until it volunteered most of its secrets, which he subsequently published in a scientific paper.

It became clear to Newton that it is impossible to escape gravity's influence and that it wasn't just Earth's inhabitants that are at the mercy of gravity's mischief. Gravity affects everything in the Universe. If gravity was suddenly turned off, the planets that were previously under gravity's spell would spin off into the far corners of the unexplored Universe, causing an uncontrollable interstellar pool game. Luckily no one has found the ON/ OFF switch for gravity yet.

But as far as we're concerned, gravity is a good sport and it generally plays ball, as long as you stick to the rules. If you take a spill when grinding down a railing,[1] two things are certain to happen: thanks to gravity you're going to end up with a broken coccyx and thanks to the inclusion of cameras in mobile phones, you're also going to end up on YouTube. But for all this fun you can have with gravity, heed a warning from Frankenstein, as gravity is capable of spawning its own monsters.[2]

WHEN WILL IT HAPPEN?	**WHEN SHOULD I START TO PANIC?**	**WHAT SHOULD I LOOK FOR?**
As long as the Earth keeps spinning on its axis and carries on orbiting the Sun then we should be fine, although gravity may send some asteroids and space debris in our direction, just for fun.	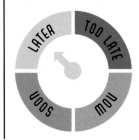	Anything from asteroids and space debris to black holes and possibly other planets. Gravity can fling whatever it likes at us, no matter what the size. Keep an eye on satellites falling from the sky too.

1. That's skate speak for 'grinding down a railing' • 2. *See* Black hole (222)

OUR **MYSTERIOUS** MISTRESS

RAVIT

INNING TO REVEAL ITS **TERRIBLE** SE

– Can you solve the ultimate conundrum?

How can something so *WEAK*

be *STRONG* enough to crush planets?

See its

Dare you

ABOLICAL
ffects on an
rdinary apple

try to escape i
POWERFU
grip?

Blk
Black hole
(222)

Black hole. *blak··whole* – a gravitational bli[...]
of space. You can't see or hear it but if you [...]
already dead.

A black hole is a classic case of when gravity goe[...]
the end of its life it can burn out and go supernov[...]
helped the star keep its shape will become its w[...]
bully the star to eat itself whole.

Once the supernova kicks in, gravity begins to [...]
ex-star into a tiny point of such concentrated ma[...]
forces become strong enough to consume everyt[...]
enough to pass by. Not even light can escape this[...]

A black hole can move through space just like [...]
hole finds a planet or two, then this ever-hung[...]
going to gobble them up like power pills. With th[...]
hiding out in the Universe it's only a matter of [...]
into our back garden and eats all our pretty flo[...]
compared to the super-massive black hole that's [...]
our galaxy. If this behemoth starts a hungry ra[...]
then let's hope it suffers indigestion after consu[...]
Saturn and Jupiter before it reaches us.

WHEN WILL IT HAPPEN?

It all depends if the sleeping giant at the centre of our Universe wakes up and decides to raid the fridge for a midnight feast.

WHAT SHOULD I LOOK FOR?

That's the problem, it's the same colour as the background it's on ...

WHEN SHOULD I START TO PANIC?

Don't sweat just yet, but even a blind squirrel will eventually find a nut.

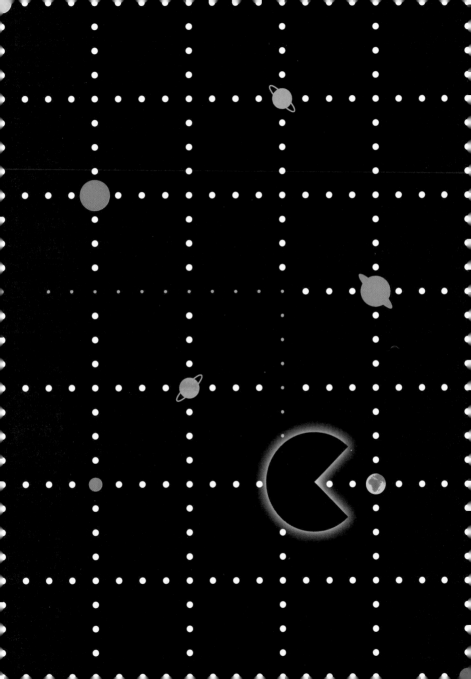

Asteroid Collision. *ass-tear-royd-col-is-thon* – when space debris strikes the Earth with varying degrees of damage: from pretty lights in the upper atmosphere to mass or total extinction.

According to NASA, at this very moment there are around 1,000 Potentially Hazardous Asteroids (PHAs) hanging out near Earth, ready to come down from the night sky to destroy you and your house. Earth is due an ass-wupping from a kick ass-teroid; after all, it's happened many times before. Asteroids are the unused building blocks of the Universe, the missing pieces of the jigsaw that have been sucked up in the vacuum. They roam through the void feeling rejected and bitter after being left out of millions of years of change while they stay dusty and unloved on their never-ending journeys. Given the length of time they spend alone, they become unpredictable, cranky and erratic, resulting in only one possible objective: a kamikaze suicide mission and the total obliteration of anything that gets in the way. These interplanetary pebbles hell-bent on destruction have witnessed many of their dusty friends' own suicide missions, including crashing into the surface of the Earth, the Moon and other such planetary objects,[2] so one can only assume that all these galactic joyrides are going to end in a spectacular pile-up. Let's just hope it's not our planet that it chooses for its final mission. But even if the

WHEN WILL IT HAPPEN?

In the next twenty-five years we're on an asteroid hit list. Look to the skies!

WHAT SHOULD I LOOK FOR?

A large flaming object in the sky that isn't usually there and isn't the Sun in a different position.

WHEN SHOULD I START TO PANIC?

Keep the pets indoors, it's almost fireworks night.

POSSIBILITY IT WILL HAPPEN?

0–100%. Depends how good its aim is.

WHAT SHOULD I DO NEXT?

Have a video camera ready to capture any space rocks that breach the Earth's atmosphere. If it doesn't wipe us out then you've got great YouTube footage.[3]

next asteroid does miss us, there is always another ready to take a shot at suicide.

asteroids

a long time ago in our galaxy far, far away ...

i love it here ...

(298)

...but i've always had a little voice inside me, wishing i'd travelled the universe more ...

d um de dum

(298)

ah well... nevermind. can't have everything. i'm happy enough here, and nothing is going to change that...

mind your backs, coming through...

(298)

i don't have the direction or the motivation to travel ...

get out of the way, blockhead !

(298)

cripes !

brace yourself !

(298)

oof !

finally ... freedom!

freedom !

you idiot ! you should look where you're turning !

what ! you came out of nowhere, there's enough space for the both of us!

(298)

quick !

we're outta here ...

run away!

taa-rah!

bye dad, i'm gonna explore the universe

(298)

bye bye son, don't get too close to anything bigger than you !

what an idiot

oh yeah! this is what it's all about

i'm going to see everything

space is ace!

a bit of personal space

with a brand-new lease of life, the 298 baptistina fragment travelled the entire solar system, visiting all the inner and outer planets time and time again and again for millennia ...

many millennia later ...

man! space is bigger than i thought!

is it possible i've seen everything there is to see ?

surely not ?

many more years later ...

hello? what's this ?

it's beautiful!

it's the most amazing thing i've seen so far !

where's the harm in that ?

maybe i'll take a closer look ...

that's close enough ...

uh oh!

ah nuts ...

everything! run away! run away !

the end

of the dinosaurs ...

XV

Aa

Asteroid attack

(226)

The Earth has taken a beating for millennia but for such a big planet the massive meteor strikes seem few and far between ... why is this and why aren't we being pummelled by meteors every day? Cut out the target below and attach it to a tree at the bottom of your garden. Walk to the other side of the garden and imagine the space between you and the target is outer space. Now borrow some darts and see how easy it is to hit the Earth.

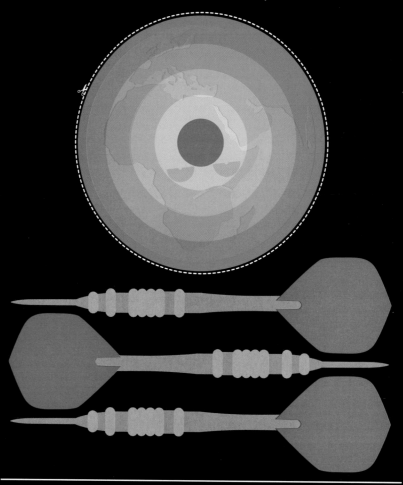

SOME ASTEROIDS OF NOTE

Asteroid A:

WHEN: 248 million years ago – Permian-Triassic boundary
SIZE: 30 miles wide
WHERE: Antarctica
CRATER NAME: Wilkes Land Crater
CRATER SIZE: 300 miles wide
RESULT: Permian-Triassic Extinction (Around 95% of all life)

Asteroid B:

WHEN: 3.47 billion years ago – Archean Period
SIZE: 12 miles wide
WHERE: Unknown: all traces of the crater have been erased
CRATER SIZE: Around 100 miles wide. Probable sea impact
RESULT: Tsunamis in every direction. Only bacteria on Earth at this stage.

Asteroid C:

NAME: Baptistina 298 Fragment
WHEN: 65 million years ago – Cretaceous -Tertiary boundary
SIZE: 6 miles wide
CRATER NAME: Chicxulub crater, Yucatan, Mexico
CRATER SIZE: 110 miles wide
RESULT: Dinosaur extinction

Asteroid D:

NAME: Tunguska event
WHEN: 30 June, 1908 - 7:17am
SIZE: Around 60 metres wide
RESULT: The object, believed to be a meteoroid, exploded above the surface of the Earth in a remote part of Siberia. An area the size of Greater London was destroyed. No reported loss of human life.

Asteroid E:

NAME: 99942 Apophis (2004 MN4)
WHEN: 13 April, 2029
SIZE: 270 metres wide
RESULT: There will be a near-miss in 2029 but it will come 10 times closer to us than our Moon. It'll have a few more attempts to hit us in 2036, 2037 and 2069.

Asteroid F:

NAME: 2000 SG 344
WHEN: September 19, 2068
SIZE: 37 metres wide
RESULT: There's around a 1 in 500 chance it will hit but it'll keep trying to hit us each year that follows ...

Source: NASA

D
E
F

0   1   2   3   4   5   6   7   8   9   10   11   12
miles

B

A

C

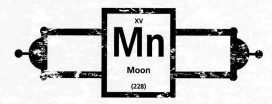

Moon. *mune* – a bright white object in the night sky. It helps us find our way to the toilet at night without turning on the light and it also covers the Sun's modesty in a total eclipse.

Without our glorious Moon shining down on us, life as we know it would be completely different. There would be no solar or lunar eclipses to confuse the birds, and no tidal system. Werewolves would not exist; but, more disturbingly, neither would we.

Some would say tidal systems are just for the surfers and the crabs, but if it wasn't for the turning of the tides then you and I would not be here in the curvy structure we all know and love. Of course we would still exist, but not in the same form. To give you an idea of what you could have been without the tides: divide your height by two, minus a few arms, add some tentacles, maybe add a few gills and you'll have imagined yourself as a whole new fish-like cognitive being. The Moon is a major factor in the tidal system. The Moon's gravity pulls our oceans away from the Earth, giving it the movement that is needed to oxygenate the life-sustaining water, which provided our fishy ancestors with an ocean of evolutionary possibilities.

But what is the future of our loyal Moon? It turns out that our dependable friend isn't as loyal as we once believed: ever since his conception he's been trying to get away from us. And how do we know this? Well, in 1969,

WHEN WILL IT HAPPEN?	WHEN SHOULD I START TO PANIC?	WHAT SHOULD I DO NEXT?
Now. I see a bad moon rising. I see trouble on the way. But don't try to catch the action, it's a very, very slow process.		Apart from tying the Moon to the Earth with massive metal cables, there isn't that much you can do to stop the Moon from leaving us. It's inevitable. But you could start work on inventing massive wave machines or sea whisks to prevent the seas from stagnating.
WHAT SHOULD I LOOK FOR?		
Dark nights and flat, calm seas. There may be a stagnant smell when you visit the seaside.	Not in your lifetime. Feel free to hit the snooze button.	

Neil Armstrong and some other Buzzards walked across the face of the **Moon.** After picnicking and enjoying the view, they failed to clear up after **themselves.** Amongst the picnic blankets and cake wrappers, they left **behind many reflective** shiny items. Back here on Earth, scientists aimed **their laser beams** directly at the Moon. The rays hit the shiny litter which **returned the beam** right back at them. By measuring the time taken for **the laser to return to Earth,** they could make an accurate measurement of

how far away the Moon is from us. After some **years and a bit** of maths, it became clear that **the Moon is trying** to escape, albeit very, VERY **slowly.** Every year the Moon retreats 3.8cm from **us.**[1] Yes, the man in the Moon has had enough **of our silly antics** and he's defecting. He's finally **decided to show us** his dark side and leave us **with an uncertain future** ... alone – the lunatic.

1. The Moon is escaping from us at about this much each year.

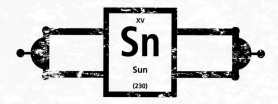

XV

Sn

Sun

(230)

Sun. *sun* – round, bright yellow object in the daytime sky. If you can see without the aid of artificial light, the Sun is probably the shiny culprit.

While the Moon is very slowly saying 'So long, suckers!', the Sun is coming towards us to embrace us with a big fiery hug.

Our Sun, which is actually a star, sprang into life about 4.6 billion years ago. With its explosive birth, a massive wind raced through the solar system, blowing away the smaller unwanted debris, leaving the larger cosmic bits and bobs behind. This was the founding of the Sun's crèche for the remaining bodies in its solar system.

Currently, the Sun is heading to the halfway point of its lifespan. If we were to think of the Sun's age in human terms, then, if the Sun were to reach the grand old age of 100, it would currently be 37.5 years old. During its middle age, the Sun will follow a similar path to us humans: its waistline will slowly expand. This expansion will be hardly noticeable to the naked eye but it will happen, and, inevitably, its belt is going to drastically slip.

By the time the Sun reaches the age of 58, it will let itself go spectacularly, it will pile on the pounds, so much so that Mercury, Venus, you, I, the Moon,[1] possibly Mars and everything in between will be engulfed by this fiery midlife crisis cannibal.[2]

WHEN WILL IT HAPPEN?	**WHEN SHOULD I START TO PANIC?**	**WHAT SHOULD I DO NEXT?**
Way past your bedtime in billions of years ...		You can sit back and earn yourself an incredibly vicious sunburn or you can start to think about how to get yourself, and the rest of the world's population, off this rock before the entire planet becomes a charred barbecued snack for the Sun.
WHAT SHOULD I LOOK FOR?		
A big orangy thing getting bigger and bigger in the sky.		
POSSIBILITY IT WILL HAPPEN?	Your suntan will be long gone before the Sun gets hungry.	
It's written in the star.		

1. If it sticks around long enough, *see* Moon (228) • 2. The Sun will start to run out of fuel: with no more hydrogen to burn, it will begin to burn up its helium and cause a rapid expansion.

I Eat Inner Planets!

At its fattest, at the age of 83, the Sun will be one massive brute with three, or possibly four, planets in its gut. But in its old age, all that will suddenly change. When the Sun reaches its twilight years, the sudden fiery amplification will stop and the weight loss that follows will be dramatic. It will experience an inability to keep warm, it'll become much weaker, it won't be as bright and, to top it all, most of its closest friends will all have died (albeit by the Sun's own hand).

The outer planets Jupiter, Saturn, Uranus and Neptune – will escape the all-you-can-eat buffet but, ultimately, their future too is black, due to the demise of their only light source. All in all, no doubt about it, it's going to end badly. Prepare to feel abandoned, hot and, finally, suffocated.

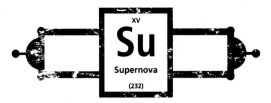

XV
Su
Supernova
(232)

Supernova. *supa·nova* – a supernova is the last **gasp of a dying** star, which can result in a colossal explosion that can **cover you and** your solar system with its cosmic entrails.

The good news is that from death comes life. New stars and planets are born from the cosmic carnage left behind by a supernova explosion. The matter that made up one such explosion is now part of your being – we are all part supernova, which is a wonderful thought. That said, the inevitable bad news is that what a supernova can give, it can also take away, with a gigantic bang. So let's not get too slushy about being made out of space dust, as another explosion can just as easily turn you back to dust in space. And with around two supernovae going off within your lifetime inside our galaxy, that's plenty more space manure in the heavens for new planets and new human races to grow in.

WHEN WILL IT HAPPEN?

When looking at stars we're looking millions of years into the past due to the light taking so long to reach us. The supernova that may finish us off could have already happened, it just hasn't reached us yet.

WHAT SHOULD I LOOK FOR?

A very bright light. The explosion will be far brighter than any other star in the sky. It may be bright enough to be visible during the day. Look for a second sun.

WHEN SHOULD I START TO PANIC?

It may already be too late. The first we'll know about it is killer gamma rays for breakfast, a large helping of radiation for lunch and planet parts for dinner. There'll be no need for pudding, as the explosion will be our just desserts.

WHICH STAR IS NEXT TO GO SUPER?

Betelgeuse, in the armpit of the Orion constellation, is ready to go supernova sometime soon,[1] if it hasn't already. The dying star that could destroy us may have already gone supernova. If it has, then the explosion will already be hurtling across millions of light years to reach us.

It may be close enough for us all to receive an unhealthy dose of gamma rays and radiation. Not so super after all.

---

1. Give or take a few hundred light years

Betelgeuse

XV
Dk
Dark matter and dark energy
(234)

Dark matter and dark energy. *darc··mat·tear··and··darc··n·ar gee* – 96% of our Universe is missing. Have you checked under the cushions? There's usually plenty of unwanted matter under there.

Space is a very mysterious place. Cosmologists have been trying to figure it out for centuries and with every couple of steps forward up the stairway to Heaven they take at least one, if not more, backwards, as every answer creates more equally hard questions.

The Universe is an infinite problem without a definitive solution and just when the Universe seems to make sense .... BANG![1] your cosmological constant goes pear-shaped. And even though cosmologists have been looking to the stars for centuries and the pieces of the jigsaw used to fit,[2] one day in the 1930s, cosmologists turned up for work, looked through their big telescopes and discovered that 96% of the Universe had gone missing overnight[3] and for the last 80 years there has been a Universal game of hide-and-seek to find out where it went.[4]

WHERE IS THE MISSING SPACE?

It is believed that the missing space is made up of dark matter and dark energy but no one has yet conclusively proved where it has gone or how it takes shape.

WHAT SHOULD I LOOK FOR?

The missing mass of the Universe that absorbs all light but doesn't reflect any and that's impossible to find against the night sky ...

WHEN SHOULD I START TO PANIC?

Not yet, as scientists don't even understand what it means, what the consequences are for the Universe or what they can do with it once it's been discovered. Does it really matter?

FACT OF THE MATTER (%)

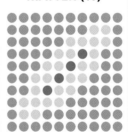

Estimates vary but approximately:
● 4% of the Universe is known
○ 26% is believed to be dark matter
● 70% is believed to be dark energy

Source: CERN

---

1. Or BOOM! ... BLAST! ... SMASH! etc ... • 2. Although some pieces fit a bit badly and had to be bashed into place • 3. Due to scientific number-crunching and cosmic estimations • 4. Scientists are even looking for this mysterious matter *inside* the Earth, a kilometre below the North Yorkshire moors within the disused Boulby potash mine.

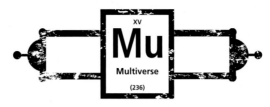

XV
Mu
Multiverse
(236)

Multiverse. *mull·tea·verse* – **only one Universe for years and then billions turn up all at once.**

A multiverse[1] is an extension of our own Universe in which each and every decision we ever make results in an alternative Universe being formed with a different outcome. The decision to work hard and keep your head down could end up in resignation in one reality or a frenzied office killing spree in another. If this is the case, then the thousands of decisions you make every day, plus the decisions of the billions of other people in the world, will form more alternative realities than grains of sand in all of the Earth's deserts put together and then some.

So if there are billions of these alternative realities in existence, where are they? They may be bubbling off the edge of our Universe, forming new ones, like a space version of frogspawn, they may be alongside our current existence right here on Earth; but we just can't see them[2] or they could exist at a quantum level,[3] but the only way to prove they exist is by visiting one. A wormhole – a rupture in time and space in the form of a reality elevator – is your best bet to venture into an alternative reality, but they're not easy to find. We suggest you try the dusty old bedroom wardrobe first. Meddling with multi-universes could open a can of wormholes. Opening the alternative door could result in an uncontrollable flood of multi-dimensional illegal immigrants crossing the alternative borders in all directions, with only one thing on their minds – actions without consequence. Multi-dimensional chaos will ensue.

WHAT SHOULD I LOOK FOR?

Look out for yourself or other duplicates for proof of multiverses. Tail your *Doppelgänger* to reveal their multi-dimensional secrets but tread carefully as this may result in a paradox[4] and we don't want that.

WHEN SHOULD I START TO PANIC?

WHAT SHOULD I DO NEXT?

Keep your discovery a secret. Experiment with actions without consequence. If it goes wrong, the alternative you will end up taking the heat instead of you as you jump through the dimension door.

1. Or parallel universe to die-hard sci-fi fans • 2. Or maybe this explains seeing your double in a crowd (or maybe it just explains ghosts) • 3. *See* Quantum mechanics (154) • 4. *See* Paradox (238)

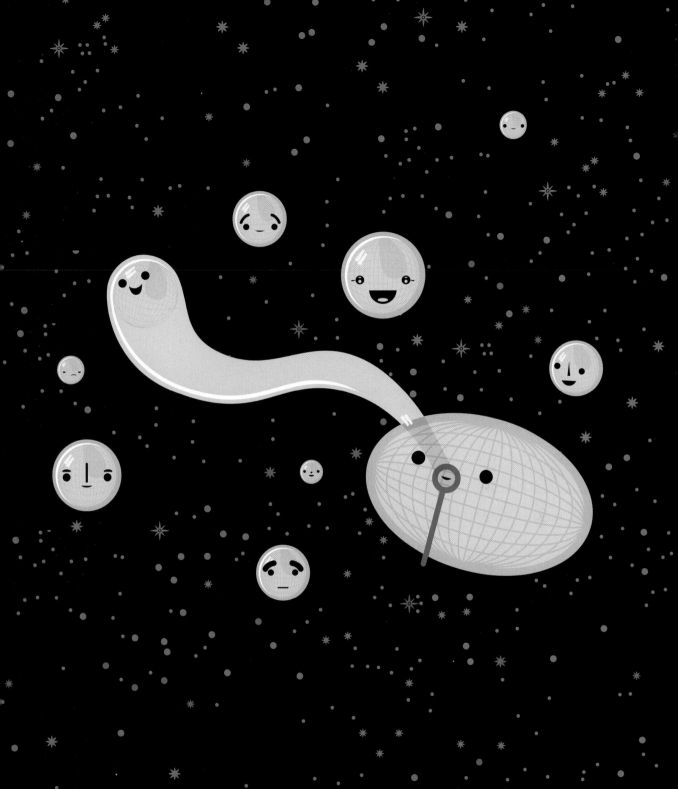

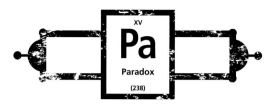

XV
Pa
Paradox
(238)

Paradox. *Parra·docks* – **a contradictory situation causing an impossible outcome, like asking a computer to save as it crashes.**

Why do you never find alternative versions of yourself invading your fridge, taking up the precious space on your sofa or sleeping with your partner while you're out at work? It's because there is an unwritten rule that, when crossing the boundaries from one multiverse to another you do not, under any circumstances, meet up with the alternative you for a few drinks. Just like Medusa's gaze, one look into the eyes of your *Doppelgänger* and everything around you will crumble like a bad *Doctor Who* special effect.

If you're lucky, only the alternative Universes will crumble, leaving one Universe behind to cope with the consequences. But if you're really unlucky, your actions will herald the end of time and space for everyone. The impossible and possible, together at last, there be the paradox.

WHAT SHOULD I LOOK FOR?

When a *Doppelgänger* looks into its double's eyes, a bad visual effect will occur resulting in the destruction of all known Universes. You'll notice an uneven green glow around you just before the surroundings begin an accelerating wobble or 'wave' motion while you stay static. People that were looking at you will now appear to be looking through you. At this point you may begin to 'wave' in the opposite direction.

WHEN SHOULD I START TO PANIC?

When you've gone back in time and accidentally killed your grandad.

WHEN WILL IT HAPPEN?

When you look into the eyes of your double, mirrors don't count. Just one look is all it took.

PARADOXICAL EXPERIMENT[1]

Things you'll need: A steel box, a vial of cyanide gas, a Geiger counter, a radioactive substance, a hammer, a trip device, a live cat.
1. Place the vial and substance in the box
2. Attach a Geiger counter, which records the decay of the radioactive substance, to the trip device which is in turn attached to the hammer placed above the vial
3. Place the cat in the box and shut the lid
4. Leave for one hour[2]

---

1. Schrödinger's cat paradox • 2. The purpose of this theoretical experiment is that you don't know whether the cat is alive or dead after the hour. The radioactive substance may decay; if it does, the Geiger counter will pick up the decay, trip the hammer to smash the vial, releasing the gas to kill the

cat. But there is an equal chance the substance will not decay. SO until we look in the box the substance has AND hasn't decayed, so the cat is both alive AND dead. It's a complicated way to kill a cat; a sack, a brick and a canal is much easier.

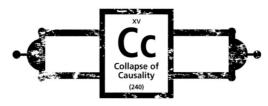

XV
Cc
Collapse of Causality
(240)

Collapse of causality. *col·lapse··ov··corz·al·ity* – when the laws that govern our everyday lives break down, causing the inversion of human civilisation.

Causality, for the time being, is behaving itself. One second following another, day following night and time will fly by as usual. All is as it should be. But start to mess around with time and you could alter the course of human history. The invention of time travel will cause a classic causality conundrum. By altering the past will we destroy the present, leaving us with no future? It's virtually guaranteed that the lure of time travel will be too great for some wacky inventors to resist sneaking a peek into the past,[1] resulting in the compromise of our very existence. Put a foot wrong in the past and it could be the beginning of the end of all of us, especially if that foot crashes down on a very special walking fish that got bored of bathing and decided to go for a look up top.

WHAT SHOULD I LOOK FOR?

People wearing unusual outfits, using strange electronic devices.

Individuals with un-traceable or conflicting backgrounds.

People that 'aren't from round these parts' that have a superior knowledge of unforeseen future world and sporting events. They will gamble and win every single time.

Individuals trying to assassinate Hitler or other world leaders. They may also be trying to prevent incidents.

WHEN SHOULD I START TO PANIC?

If you see the crackle of electricity coming from someone's garage or you see reverse lightning on a cloudless day, get ready to worry. If that same person travels back and alters your family tree, there's no time to panic, you'll just cease to be.

WHAT SHOULD I DO NEXT?

Although the prospect of time travel is an attractive one, proceed with caution.

Time travel can only cause you problems because by travelling to the past you alter the future, so it will be impossible for you to return to the exact 'future' you came from.

As far as present-day time travellers are concerned, if time travel was possible, wouldn't our present already be full of time travel tourists?

---

1. If time travel becomes possible you will only be able to travel back in time from the point you turn the machine on and not forward. How can you go into a future that hasn't happened yet?

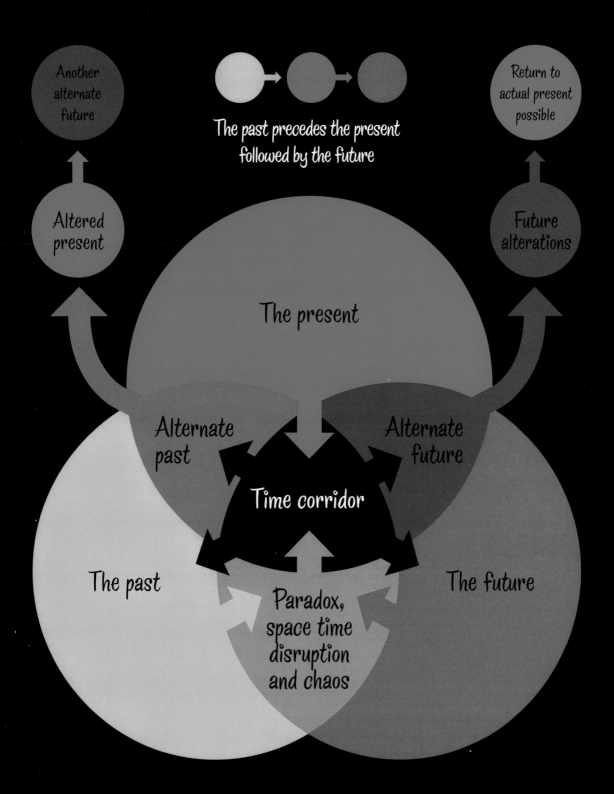

Vacuum metastability. *vac·qume··met·ass·stab·bill·it·tee* – the unstable vacuum of space is ready to start spring cleaning.

The vacuum of space is like a cracked Thermos flask. You can enjoy your favourite hot (or cold) drink as usual, time after time, but then one day ... BOOM!!!!! – you'll suddenly be wearing the beverage of your choice rather than drinking it.

The reason for the explosion is that the open flask will cause the glass to heat up or cool down, making the glass to expand or contract, which, in turn, over time, will cause the explosion. Our Universe could suffer a similar fate, although the only difference is that, rather than being covered in cold gazpacho, the Earth will become covered with the entire contents of the Universe's vacuum dust-bag. So when the vacuum starts its cleaning there won't even be enough time to lift your feet off the floor.

WHEN WILL IT HAPPEN?

The failure of the vacuum in space could happen at any time.

Space isn't as stable as was once thought, so one second you're alive, and the next second, bang, you're dead.

WHAT SHOULD I LOOK FOR?

Signs of life. If you're conscious and you can see, feel, taste, smell and hear then the vacuum hasn't failed ... yet.

If the Sun is still shining then the vacuum is still working.

WHEN SHOULD I START TO PANIC?

When it does happen it'll already be too late to panic – the vacuum will have finished its deadly spring clean as soon as it's begun.

We're living on very borrowed time: it's a miracle we're actually still here at all.

WHAT WILL HAPPEN NEXT?

Once the vacuum has enveloped everything in the entire Universe it could collapse on itself to create the perfect ingredients for another big bang. Some believe that the explosion that kick started this Universe was the result of this type of vacuum explosion.

So the ultimate end of the Universe as we know it may be the birth of an entirely new Universe where life may, or may not, flourish.

Hey! Do you want to try out my new Thermos flask?
Yeah sure
Whoa! What's all that stuff coming out of it?
Not sure ... maybe the vacuum's broken
I've got planets in my tea now. Do you still have the receipt?

Sd
XV
Space dust
(244)

Space dust. *spayse··dust –* Earth to Earth, ashes to ashes, dust to dust ...

If it wasn't for the first bacteria that began to thrive 3.5 billion years ago then we wouldn't be around today, but maybe earthly bacteria weren't the first link in the human evolution story after all. Are we the product of spontaneous bacterial growth or did we get a kick start from somewhere else? During our planet's early years, the building blocks of life could have been deposited here after a dust-up with asteroid impacts during Earth's formation. The dusty elements from the asteroid could have mixed together with Earth's ingredients and *voilà,* an all-new recipe for an evolutionary line based on alien genes. If we are the product of extra-terrestrial genes from hitch-hiking space dust, then asteroids would have also bombarded other planets, leaving behind their dirty cargo – could this mean there may be a whole host of our alien relatives on distant rocky outcrops for us to reacquaint ourselves with? (Although their own evolutionary legacy may have taken a very different line to ours.) If we are born of space dust what's to say that it won't happen again? Could we be affected by another dusty space rock, this time featuring a violent space disease? We'll have to wait and see ... here's a killer species they prepared earlier.

WHEN WILL IT HAPPEN?

Hopefully it won't happen nowadays. Since the early bombardments of the Earth, an atmosphere has formed around our planet; it's like an electric fence against invading threats. Any alien dust hitch-hiking on an asteroid, should cook in the atmosphere.

WHEN SHOULD I START TO PANIC?

Not yet, especially since it might be the reason that you're here.

WHAT SHOULD I LOOK FOR?

Friends and family suffering from illnesses with symptoms you don't recognise after bright lights have been spotted in the sky.

EARTH-LIKE COPIES

It's possible that there may be up to 100 billion planets similar to Earth in our galaxy alone ...

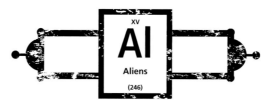

XV
Al
Aliens
(246)

Aliens. *a·leons* – a non-human form that has come to befriend us, enslave us, hump us or kill us, or all four, and not necessarily in that order.

When an alien race does finally reveal itself to us, they're in for a hostile reception. Aliens have already taken a thrashing from the human race through the B-movies of the twentieth century. In those visions of the future we get knocked down and we get up again and then we kick their little green asses back to the dark and insignificant corner of the Universe that they call home. But while we stand in the rubble of our once magnificent cities, we've only got ourselves to blame.

How so? Well, we can't blame the aliens if they come in peace but leave us in pieces, as we've basically been asking for it. We've been broadcasting our B-movie propaganda for the last century: that if any alien sets foot[1] on our Earth, they'll find themselves going home in a photon ambulance.

Any passing alien that picks up these signals will witness the attacks on our planet by various alien species,[2] the perpetual destruction of cities like New York and London, followed by the eventual annihilation of countless hostile alien races that have threatened Earth.

On the one hand it's the perfect KEEP OUT sign but on the other hand we're broadcasting a message to the cosmos to 'Come and have a go if you think you're hard enough'.

These movies have put us on the defensive, while the TV signals that are being carried into the cosmos for everyone (or everything) to see are the equivalent of unsecured internet access to the aliens: the perfect search engine for knowing your enemy.[3] The history of the Earth is at their thingertips – they'll know our weapons and the weapons' weaknesses, our cultural similarities and differences, resulting in the perfect invasion plan.

So with our suspicion of anything alien,[4] when we do encounter an alien life form, we're in for one hell of a rumble. All we have to do is find their hiding place first ...

---

1. Or the alien equivalent to a foot (for example, is the Blob omnipedal or is it one singular foot?)
2. Convincing (and unconvincing) • 3. But not through shows like *Jerry Springer* unless the subject is

WE ARE NOT YOUR FRIENDS, WE MEAN YOU HARM

WHEN WILL IT HAPPEN?

We haven't found any little green men hiding 'out there' so far (according to our government) but the aliens may have already found us.

As it takes millions of light years to reach us, there could be an alien landing party on its way to investigate us already. It's only a matter of time ... and distance.

You'd better set an extra place at the dinner table, we're expecting uninvited guests.

WHAT SHOULD I LOOK FOR?

A complexion of green or skin that doesn't fall into the 'normal' colour categories. Lights in the sky. Anyone trying to fit in but failing miserably.

WHEN SHOULD I START TO PANIC?

They might already be amongst us ...

POSSIBILITY IT WILL HAPPEN?

Around 1.5% of Americans claim aliens have already been assimilated into our society and that the government is run by aliens. Other say they've been abducted and operated on by aliens and many claim to have married one.

Source: The Roper Poll

along the lines of 'Is the president an alien?' • 4. Unless you're the intergalactic sex ranger, Captain James T. Kirk – suspicious of no one, special friend to all and who will do anything to anything

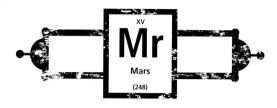

Mars. *marz* – the only planet in the solar system that we can turn into an extension of Earth. Think of Mars as a kind of space shed at the end of the garden.

We used to have high hopes for life on Mars but with the photographing of the entire surface of Mars in 1965 by the Mariner 4 probe, it was revealed that our hopes were unfounded as no settlements were spotted, no glass domes were uncovered and there weren't even any flying saucers. All that was revealed was a cold and barren red rock. Mars had let us down.

It looked like the chances of anything coming from Mars were millions to one. But then the search shifted from the red planet back down to our blue one, and rather than looking for little green men, the emphasis was shifted to little red rocks here on Earth. In 1996 a rock was uncovered in Antarctica and was given the absurd name of named Allan Hills.[1] This little rock revealed that there had, at one time, been life on Mars;[2] the red planet was cool again. But with all this euphoria and rush to get men on Mars, the threat from Martians is still real, albeit a threat from a very small and un-green source. Just like space dust[3] this Martian bacteria may be our very undoing. When humankind has established itself on the red rock and areas of the planet have been cultivated, the once dormant bacteria that have been accidentally resurrected may begin to thrive in the warm spacesuit of an unsuspecting gardener. One lung full of newly resurrected alien spores may be all it takes before the Martians finally get their revenge.

WHEN WILL IT HAPPEN?	WHEN SHOULD I START TO PANIC?	WHAT SHOULD I DO NEXT?
NASA hopes to send a manned mission to Mars by 2030, unless scientists who've handled Allan become ill first.		Don't be the first to sign up for life on Mars. Wait to see how the early settlers get on. If no strange illnesses materialise, then volunteer for the move as planned; if people do turn green around the gills, run a million miles.
WHAT SHOULD I LOOK FOR?		
Frothing at the mouth and a green skin tinge.	We have to get there first.	

1. Full name Allan Hills 84001, or ALH 84001 for short. Named after the mountain range in Antarctica where it was discovered • 2. Although the rock had been on Earth's surface for millions of years, so the organism may have been from Earth all along: they're still fighting about that one • 3. *See* Space dust (244)

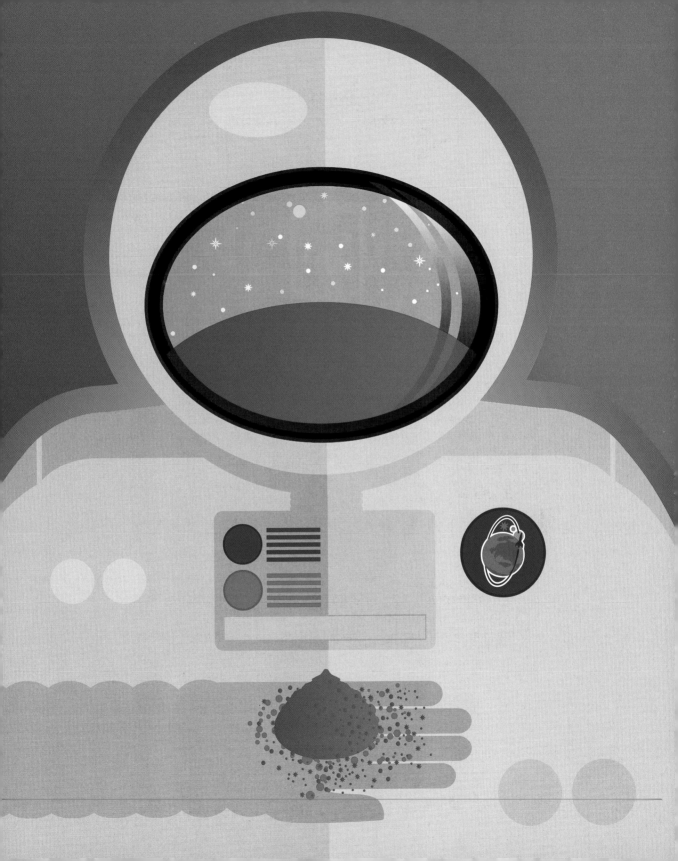

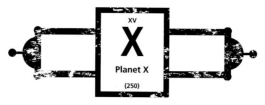

XV
X
Planet X
(250)

Planet X *plan·et··ex* – a planet set to enter our solar system, giving science-textbook editors many a headache.

In 2006, our solar system was subject to a cosmic audit. Cosmologists took stock of everything in our solar system, from the big gassy planets to the insignificant rocks. It was discovered that, for the last 75 years, Pluto had been labelled incorrectly; the solar system was reordered, resulting in Pluto being renamed 'dwarf planet' and consigned to the lower shelf of history. At the end of the stocktake, nine planets became eight, and two more dwarf planets were discovered hidden under the space couch. But the thing about space is that it doesn't stay still for a second and objects move in and out of the solar system at will, including planets.

Planet X (aka Nibiru) is the next planet that is believed to be gatecrashing our solar system. Some believe that the planet could be about the size of Mars, others imagine it to be like Jupiter with a glandular problem, but most believers in Planet X agree that the scientific community have been keeping this elusive space wanderer a secret.[1]

As for its orbit, when Planet X does make an appearance, it's going to barge its way through the solar system making a beeline for Earth, causing massive strains on its gravity, culminating in earthquakes, volcanic activity, a change in the Earth's orbit and, ultimately, destruction. A substitute for Pluto it is not.

WHEN WILL IT HAPPEN?

Planet X was due to pass by a few years ago. It has now been pencilled in for an Earth drive-by in 2012.[2]

X MARKS THE SPOT

Expect excellent extra-terrestrial excitement.

WHEN SHOULD I START TO PANIC?

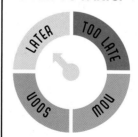

WHAT SHOULD I LOOK FOR?

A massive great planet in the sky hoving into your view and blocking out all the sunlight.

SHOULD I WORRY?

Stick to worrying about aliens, they're far more likely.

---

1. They've done really well: it would take a lot of black blankets to hide an entire planet • 2. Date subject to change, watch this space

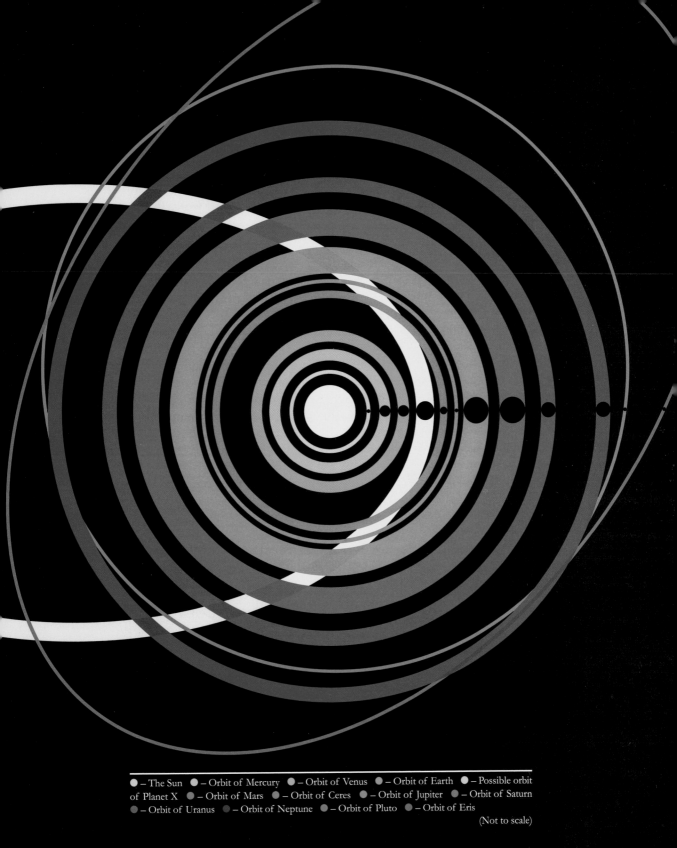

● – The Sun ● – Orbit of Mercury ● – Orbit of Venus ● – Orbit of Earth ● – Possible orbit of Planet X ● – Orbit of Mars ● – Orbit of Ceres ● – Orbit of Jupiter ● – Orbit of Saturn ● – Orbit of Uranus ● – Orbit of Neptune ● – Orbit of Pluto ● – Orbit of Eris

(Not to scale)

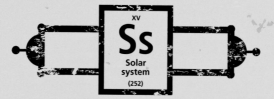

Ss

XV

Solar system

(252)

Solar system. *so·la··sis·tum* – the world in which our world lives.

The solar system has been Earth's home for the last 4.6 million years and it has still to give up all its secrets. We know that the Moon is deserting us, the Sun is going to eat us and any decent-sized lump of rock could catch us off guard and kill us all, but what of our fellow planets, dwarf planets and/or plutoids? Surely we're safe from them? Well, this may not be the case after all.

Our cosmically constant companions of Mercury, Venus, Mars, Jupiter, Saturn, Uranus and Neptune and all our newly categorised friends have been our seemingly unchanging space amigos since the Sun exploded into life, sweeping the solar system of the smaller dust and debris that littered our backyard. But there is one of our comrades that's starting to get a bit twitchy. The familiar swirls of clouds of Jupiter's exterior, like a Christmas jumper, are changing. New bands are appearing on its surface and scientists are not sure why. The planet that is famous for its spots is beginning to develop a few more and it's got scientists concerned that it may be going through a tough time, internally. One theory claims that deep inside Jupiter's swirly exterior, the already gassy planet has to endure explosive thermonuclear reactions that may, one day, result in the planet's

WHEN WILL IT HAPPEN?	WHEN SHOULD I START TO PANIC?	A LOOK INTO THE SYSTEM (%)

WHEN WILL IT HAPPEN?

Who knows? Jupiter is going through a period of change that has never been witnessed before.

WHAT SHOULD I LOOK FOR?

The big gas giant letting go and spreading its gassy fumes in our direction.

WHEN SHOULD I START TO PANIC?

It's already too late: we need to cross our fingers and hope for the best.

A LOOK INTO THE SYSTEM (%)

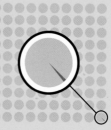

99.8% of the solar system is taken up by the Sun
● the remaining 0.2% contains everything else

Source: NASA

1. The Red spot is a swirling super storm that has been raging for centuries

stomach exploding its contents over Earth, killing us all.

It may just be another bad case of wind,[1] as some suspect that Jupiter is experiencing a period of climate change. We'll just have to wait and see if the bloated planet blows a gasket or not.

Know your enemy

The Sun

Power: **Heat and Light**
Weapon: **Life Giver and Taker**

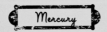

Mercury

Power: **Speed**
Weapon: **Offensive Messages**

Venus

Power: **Seduction**
Weapon: **Love and Lust**

Mars

Power: **Warmonger**
Weapon: **Armoured Vehicles**

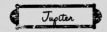

Jupiter

Role: **Commander in Chief**
Power: **Enormous Strength**
Weapon: **Natural Leader**

Saturn

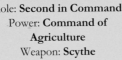
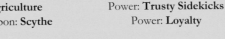

Role: **Second in Command**
Power: **Command of Agriculture**
Weapon: **Scythe**

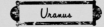

Uranus

Power: **Command of the Skies**
Weapon: **Zeppelins**

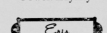

Moons

Power: **Trusty Sidekicks**
Power: **Loyalty**

Neptune

Power: **Command of the Sea**
Weapon: **Trident**

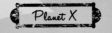

Asteroids & Comets

Power: **Element of Surprise**
Weapon: **Nuclear Transference**

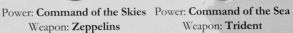

Pluto

Power: **Deception**
Weapon: **Chameleon-like Properties**

Ceres

Power: **Command of the Seasons**
Weapon: **Instability**

Eris

Power: **Sower of Strife and Discord**
Weapon: **Invisibility**

Planet X

Power: **Stealth**
Weapon: **Element of Surprise**

Please note: Planets and Sun to scale excluding Moons, Asteroids and Planet X. The Earth is approximately the same size as Venus

XVI
Appendix

Appendix. *app·end·dicks* – the section of a book named after the organ in the body that you don't really need.

The appendix section of a book is like the last words of a dying man: a scrambled and random selection of final thoughts that are supposed to help you come to terms with the rapidly approaching end before the chapter finally draws to a close.

The appendix is generally a collection of random titbits within the twilight pages of the book. It contains the leftover bits and bobs that couldn't be levered into the main body of the book.

The appendix is sometimes informative but usually dull. The reader can usually be forgiven for skipping this section.

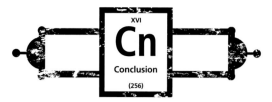

XVI
Cn
Conclusion
(256)

Conclusion. *con·clue·shon* – **the end of 'the end of the world' scenarios in a concise and final thought.**

Earth has coped pretty well over the last 4.6 billion years in the cold and loneliness of space. It has survived more attempts to knock it off its perch than a very lucky coconut in a 24-hour coconut-shy record attempt.[1] Luckily for us, nothing has yet succeeded in winning the sorry-looking cuddly toys on offer[2] and that's because the Earth is one lucky son of a Sun of a bitch[3] – it had to hone its survival skills rather quickly.

If the history of the Universe was expressed as a calendar, with the big bang occurring on the very first second of 1 January and present day being midnight on 31 December, Earth would have formed on 14 September while humans would appear just after lunchtime on New Year's Eve. We have only had to survive since the one o'clock news and we're already moaning, while the Earth has managed to last well over fifteen weeks[4] out in the wilderness of a Universal assault course, braving the very worst that the cosmos has to throw at it. So while our planet can take a lot of heat, we humans can't. There may be almost 7 billion of us but there's only one of it, and Earth is a better man that mankind is. He's been on our side in many fist fights with the Universe. However, when it comes to our own man-made issues or Acts of God, we're on our own. All good things must come to an end[5] and there is a very big chance that we humans will finish the race far earlier that Earth will. In this case, second best *is* very best.

WHAT SHOULD I DO NEXT?	THE LAST DAY ON EARTH	MUSIC AT HUMAN-KIND'S FUNERAL
Plan ahead. The robots may have already organised their uprising and economic collapse may render us penniless but if you can anticipate the problems then you're one step ahead of the cannon fodder.	Things To Do on the last day: buy something expensive that you couldn't afford before or give all your money away, settle old scores, sleep through it, sleep with someone through it, visit family, get drunk and party!	The Doors: 'The End', R.E.M: 'It's the End of the World as We Know It (And I Feel Fine)', Queen: 'Another One Bites the Dust', David Bowie: 'Ashes to Ashes', The Smiths 'I Know it's Over'

1. *See* Asteroid collision • 2. Although Theia, the planet that collided with the Earth, came close except she didn't survive to claim her prize • 3. *See* Sun (230) • 4. Although Earth has had a head start, as it needed to tidy up before we arrived • 5. And thankfully, many bad things too

Draw your own conclusion. *draw··yor··own··con·clue·shon –* how do you think the world will end? Draw your own conclusions below.

WHEN WILL IT HAPPEN?	WHEN SHOULD WE START TO PANIC?	WHAT SHOULD WE LOOK FOR?

WHEN WILL IT HAPPEN?

In the spaces provided add the year you predict the world will end

... and the number of human lives lost

WHEN SHOULD WE START TO PANIC?

LATER • TOO LATE • SOON • NOW

WHAT SHOULD WE LOOK FOR?

1.

1. Cut out the arrow and place it on the panic chart to indicate when you believe the end of the world will come

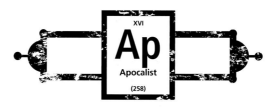

XVI

Ap

Apocalist

(258)

Apocalist. *ap·ock·ah·list* – when the end of days begin, you'll need to rely on the stockpile of items you've been storing in your bulging basement.

Some Essentials

At least one member
  of the opposite sex
Axe
Ball of string
Batteries,
  various sizes
Blankets
Bottled water
Candles
Change of clothes
Compass
Diary
Disguises, various
Emergency flares
First-aid kit
Footwear,
  various types

Gas canisters
Gas masks
Gas stoves
Generator
Guitar
Lie detector
Maps
Matches
Medication
Money
Petrol
Radiation suit
Refrigeration device
Reliable vehicle
Safe house
Tin foil
Tin opener
Tinned food

Torch
Trustworthy friends
Variety of weapons,
  including shot guns
Water, as much as
  possible

Skills

Ingenuity
Leadership skills
Map-reading skills
Survival skills
  (inc. firelighting)

Optional

An Ark
Antidotes for
  various diseases

WHAT SHOULD I DO NEXT?

Gather together as many of the items on the list as you can, hide them away in a secret underground bunker, tell no one of its whereabouts and sit back and wait for the apocalypse to come to you.

WHEN SHOULD I START TO PANIC?

IN THE EVENT OF YOUR DEATH

Sign the declaration and will on page 261 and keep it hidden upon your person at all times. Where you hide it is up to you. In death your legacy will live on and your secret stash will not be wasted.

Die. *dye* (singular) **or Dice.** *dyz* (plural) – whether you live or die is down to the dice of fate.[1]

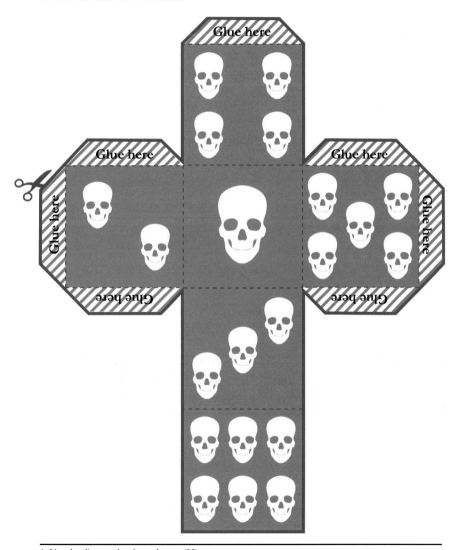

1. Use the dice to play Apocalysmo (32)

Die. *dye* (singular) or **Dice.** *dys* (plural) – whether you live or die is down to the dice of fate.

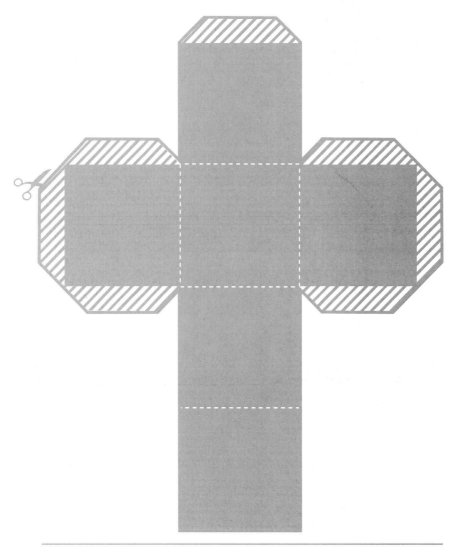

I, the undersigned, declare that in the forthcoming Apocolypse:
• I will be prepared for whatever **Doomsday / Judgment Day / Alien Invasion Day / Nuclear War Day** may bring.
• I will fight to the best of my abilities for my fellow man against aliens, killer robots, risen machines, Satan, the Four Horsemen of the Apocalypse, the hounds of Hell or other such monsters that have been unleashed against the human race.
• I will never give up the good fight unless I am aware of my own limitations such as rashes and seizures brought on by man-made viruses, or drooling and limb loss due to zombification. In case of this event I will dispatch myself.
• I will not leave anyone behind. I will kill my friends and family only if I suspect that they have been infected by a global pandemic, killer virus, if they start to show signs of monsterism or join the enemy.
• In the event of the collapse of the human population, I will attempt to revitalise the human race as often as physically possible.

LAST WILL AND TESTAMENT

I revoke all previous wills for this is my final and one true will. Everything I own, including my weapons store, stash of viral antidotes, vehicles and secret bunker, I hereby leave to _____ in the event of my death.

Write your final last words here:

_____

_____

_____

Sign   Date

XVI

Cn

Confession

(262)

I, the undersigned, confess my sins in the vain hope of saving my soul
(write your confession in the space provided):

_____   _____

Sign   Date

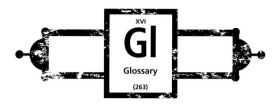

Glossary. *gloss·ary* – words and terms that will help you survive an intelligent dinner party conversation about the end of the world or green issues.

Aghast.

ag·ast – the term used for the first sharp intake of breath when you realise your gas mask isn't working properly

Animalady.

an·emal·lad·dee – a sick animal

Anticipointment.

ann·tiss·e·poynt·ment – the build-up to eventual disappointment

Apocalapse.

ap·ock·ah·lapz – when the scheduled end of the world doesn't materialise. *See* Mayan calendar: 2012 (146)

Apocalist.

ap·ock·ah·list – the list of essential items you need to see you through the nightmare that is about to ensue

Chaosity.

kay·os·city – the ensuing panic that comes with the realisation that the end is here, and no longer nigh

CLI mate.

clye·mate – a friend of the Earth who is part of the Clean Living Institute

Climate change.

cly·mate··ch·ayng – when you fall out with your clean-living friend

Coffing.

koff·fing – the final wheezing before inevitable death

Credit crunch.

ker·red·it··ker·unch – when the cost of your breakfast cereal rises due to the economic crisis

Doommonger.

dume·mun·ger – a purveyor of doom and gloom

Doommongrel.

dume·mun·ger·el – 1. the hell hounds owned by a doommonger 2. A doommonger that pushes incorrect facts about the end of the world

Foke.
foke – the original name for smog, derived from 'Fog' and 'smoke'.
See Pollution (108)

Freediction.
free·dick·shon – the process of altering a long-established prediction to fit a situation.
See Modern-day Nostrodami (148)

Greenhouse gases.
grene·houze··gas·ez – the stale air caused by flatulent vegetation that becomes trapped in the glass house at the bottom of the garden

Phood.
phood – food that has been exposed to radiation

Pry mate.
pri·mate – a so-called 'friend' who wants to know all your monkey business

Mankey.
man·key – an ill monkey.
See Animal zoonosis (98)

Nigh mare
nigh·mare – a horse of the apocalypse. *See* Four Horsemen (30)

Quing and Keen.
kw·ing··and··keyne – asexual or hermaphroditic king and queen
See Warming seas (106)

Seacosystem.
see·coe·sis·tem — an underwater ecosystem

Sofasayer.
sow·far·say·ya — An armchair soothsayer

Skulk.
scu·hulk – a moody-looking skull

Stem cell
stem·sel — A jail for dissected steam

Skulk.
scu·hulk – a moody-looking skull

Late additions.
layt··ad·dish·chons – other apocalyptic words, sayings and phrases. Add your own below.

_____

_____

_____

_____

_____

_____

_____

_____